Vera Forster was present at some of the most significant events in recent history. A Jewish teenager in pre-war Hungary, she was seventeen when Hitler invaded Poland. At nineteen, she was in hiding in Budapest. With a new identity, she worked for an underground group forging papers until arrested by the Gestapo. At the age of twenty she was learning how to survive in Auschwitz. By the time the Allied forces arrived in Berlin, she had been liberated by the Russians and was dancing the polka with other survivors in a rococo villa in Warsaw.

She returned to a Hungary which had become a Soviet satellite, to find that, from being a persecuted Jew, she had become a bourgeois class enemy. Shortly after graduating from university, she was pushing wheelbarrows on a building site. After Stalin died, she became a lecturer at the National Drama School and joined her students on the protest march of October 23rd 1956, which triggered the Hungarian Revolution. When the Revolution failed, she left Hungary for Austria and eventually, England, where she has lived and worked for nearly half a century.

The triumph of the human spirit was never more engagingly told than it is in this story of one woman's life in the most turbulent of times.

A Daughter of Her Century

First published in the UK 2009 by The Clucket Press
reprinted 2010

Conditions of sale

Typeset in Adobe Garamond Pro by Niall Horn, The Clucket Press

Printed and bound in the UK by CPI Antony Rowe, Chippenham, Wiltshire

British Library Cataloguing in Publication Data
A CIP catalogue record for this book is available from the British Library

ISBN-13: 978-0-9549256-8-0

The Clucket Press
220 Hill Lane, Southampton, Hants SO15 7NR

www.tattybogle.com

A Daughter of Her Century

Vera Forster

The Clucket Press

Acknowledgements

My thanks to Niall Horn, the magician who turned my text into this book.

***

We are very grateful to George Szirtes for permission to quote from his translation of the poem by Gyula Juhász.

***

Versions of some of the stories have previously been published in magazines including The London Review, Metropolitan and Paperclip

For 'The Writers';
Valerie, Sandra, Jayne and Henrietta…

and, of course, for Harry.

My thanks also to Gwyneth Roberts
for her encouragement and active help.

With best wishes,
[illegible]

Contents

Part One

BEGINNINGS

1

A clever child chooses well the time and place to be born. Márton Street in Budapest in 1924 was not the best choice. My parents already had a sixteen year old daughter for whom, eventually, a dowry would have to be found and nothing was further from their minds than wanting another child.

'Mother had thought that it was her time of life,' my sister later recalled, 'when she found out, there was nothing we could do about it.'

'What do you mean, 'do about it?' I cried, 'You're talking about me!'

I, who was the centre of the Márton Street universe, the little princess who had the top of the milk saved for her every day and went to a German speaking nursery school. I, who was my mother's darling, but had to learn the bitter necessities of life, sitting on the potty for hours when she was too busy in the shop to give me the word of release. What would she have done without me? What would her sister Aunt Helen talk about when she visited her, if not me? Whom would mother have taken to Grandmother on her Sunday visits if I were not there?

According to my sister, the news of my mother's pregnancy was a terrible shock to them. Besides the nuisance of a baby, it was the indisputable proof that she and my father still… It didn't bear thinking about. She was, for Heaven's sake, thirty-nine! Surely she shouldn't be walking on the street showing herself in that condition to the neighbours? 'Yet,' said my sister, 'when she first saw the newborn baby, her fear and shame took a sudden twist and turned into love.'

'It's hard to believe that you were the baby I hated so much,' she said affectionately and kissed me, 'I can't imagine now what I would do without you!'

Something similar must have happened to my mother because I know that she loved me. A few years ago, almost by miracle, I found some letters written by her to her sister Aunt Helen when I was two years old. 'Vera has charmed everyone, she is such a darling.' 'She is very bright and talks like a three year old.' She was proud of me, but I was the constant source of her anxiety. Did the child eat enough? Shouldn't she be asleep? 'You mustn't let her talk to strange children in the park!'

As for my father, it is difficult to imagine how he reacted to the news. He probably whistled softly to himself and went in search of a cigarette.

Márton Street, where I was born, was paved with cobblestones and the street lamps blinked in surprise at their newly introduced electricity. The houses stood cheek by jowl, but no two of them were alike. Some of them had two windows, heavily lidded with drop shutters and a doorway large enough to swallow a horse and a cart. Others had a mean little entrance with only one window on the front, like a one-eyed ogre. The house in which we lived had a large wooden gateway with a smaller door cut into it. It led to a cobbled courtyard flanked by flats on both sides. Our flat was larger that the rest. We had two rooms, one with a window to the street, to which a smaller room was added as my sister Marinka was growing up. She was thrilled with it until – alas! – she had to share it with a baby.

Ours was the best flat because the house was owned by my father's parents who lived nearby in Tüzoltó Street. It was my mother's great grievance that, when Grandmother Forster came to collect the monthly rent, she also collected it from us. What kind of Jewish mother was it who would not allow her son to live rent-free in her house?

Her own mother, Grandmother Schönbaum, had also lived in the Márton Street house before I was born, and so had my mother's sister, Aunt Helen, and their brother, Nandor. Now listen to this: Aunt Helen and Nandor were my father's cousins because my two grandmothers were sisters. My father and mother were first cousins, so that Grandmother Forster was not only my mother's mother-in-law, she was also her aunt. Nobody I knew had such a complicated family.

But this was not the only thing which made me special; I also had flaming red hair. Not a single one of the children in the neighbourhood had red hair. Grandmother Forster, in whose youth this had been regarded as a sign of bad temper, once confessed that her white hair used to be similar to mine and suggested the use of walnut oil, but my mother laughed and said that we liked my hair as it was.

I have always envied people who knew about their origins. I know very little about my two grandmothers and even less about their husbands who came to Budapest in the 1850's from somewhere in the north of Hungary. I was not allowed even to know in what language the two grannies talked to each other.

'A German dialect,' said my mother, who was ashamed of her parents' *Yiddish*. We were emancipated Jews who had no time for the superstitious ways of the ghetto and only limited time for God. The High Holiday had to be honoured because it was then that God decided what would happen to you during the coming year, but since He did not seem to bother about my mother's cooking, dairy products got increasingly mixed up with meat dishes.

What were they like, my family? They lived in their present, which was the culmination of everything that had happened in their past. They were enlightened, having learnt about germs and vitamins, and my mother was the first in the family to have a telephone installed in the tiny entrance hall. Like generations before and after them, they didn't know much about each other, but they knew exactly what was what. Fur coats in the wardrobe had to be put into camphor for the summer, to prevent their producing moths, and children had to be controlled to prevent them becoming selfish. If you shaved a girl's head it made her hair grow; if you prevented her from curling up in sleep, she would grow nice and tall. The Christians were given too much to drink and believed in Jesus who was a great man, but by no means God, since the one and only God was ours. Poverty was vaguely shameful. You could have two scrambled eggs, but never three, whereas jam-filled pancakes came in threes; nobody could have two or four.

What they never talked about was sex. Even the words 'male' or 'female' were anathema to my mother. The world consisted of men and women, gentlemen and ladies. Animals presumably had no gender. My insistence that not all babies could have been brought by the storks, which left the country for the winter, was met by giggles from my sister Marinka, and a stern rebuke from my mother who found my interest premature. The word 'pregnant' was never used; big bellies were something a child was not supposed to notice nor ask about. Men had certain urges to which women had to submit, 'but it happens in the dark and afterwards you'll manage to forget it,' my Aunt Helen promised me many years later.

Instead of sex they talked about money. Love and hate, exploitation and dependence, masqueraded as matters of money. Wives complained that what their husbands provided was not enough, husbands complained about excessive demands, as if they were talking in code. Poverty was impotence. Real men made money.

The 'real man' in my family was my mother's bank manager brother Nandor. By the time I was born he'd moved from Márton Street to a fashionable part of the city where he lived with Grandmother Schönbaum and his sister Aunt Helen. From the vantage point of Márton Street he was rich as Croesus. He provided Aunt Helen with a dowry for her second marriage, sent his mother regularly to an elegant spa in Margit Island on the Danube and paid for my education. My father hated him, which probably influenced the short story which I, his ungrateful niece, wrote for a magazine many decades later.

Uncle Nandor - a story.

At the age of ten I'd written a poem. I can still quote the first verse although it might have lost something in translation.

'The purple sunset, O behold!
Transforms the corn to molten gold,
Silvery clouds cast a shadow
On the emerald of the meadow.'

Everyone said it was a very colourful poem. I'd shown it to several members of my family who all liked it. I thought of trying my hand at writing a novel as well but it was too late. The school year had ended and I was sent to a holiday camp.

It was not a proper camp, only a villa on the outskirts of Budapest run by Mrs Feher, whose advertisement in the papers promised healthy food and sports facilities for girls aged between ten and fifteen. It was a disappointment. The food tasted of nothing but vitamins, and the sports facilities consisted of the nearby wood. After breakfast the dining room was transformed into a gymnasium. Mr Feher, a retired PE teacher, would stand in the middle with something like castanets in his hand beating the time. 'One-two-three, one-two-three. Back up straight, lift your knees.' He'd glare at me with distaste because my elasticised black gym pants would keep slipping down and I always missed the beat.

One morning while we were getting dressed in the dormitory an older girl rushed in waving a newspaper at me.

'It's been published! Your poem has been published!' She was followed by Mrs Feher and the matron. Everyone gathered round me to look at the paper. It was folded to show the bottom of the third page where the last column bore the title: Young Poetess Shows Great Promise.

Underneath the article was my poem printed in full, with my name below. Manci, my temporary best friend in the camp, tore the paper from my hand and began to read it aloud.

'Young poetess shows great promise.' She stopped and looked at me enviously.

'The Evening Echo couldn't resist printing this poem written by the orphaned niece of Bank Manager Nandor Schönbaum. Mr Schönbaum, whose name is well known in financial circles, contributes generously to the upbringing of his nine-year-old niece. Mr. Schönbaum's magnanimity as the patron and benefactor of young talent is clearly not misplaced.'

I stood dumbfounded, like somebody hit on the head by the rainbow's pot of gold. Although I was too young to speculate how much money the journalist owed or needed to borrow from Uncle Nandor, I felt the shadow of a doubt. Was my poem really that good? It must have been, everyone was smiling and shaking my hand. Mrs Feher patted my shoulder and said that she was very proud of me and that I could use the spare room next door whenever I wanted to write poems. Just to let her know when I felt inspired, and she'd give me the key.

'I feel it now,' I said, 'Can I please be excused from the morning drill?'

But inspiration had deserted me. Had Uncle Nandor been asked at the Pearly Gates to enumerate his good deeds on earth he would have been well advised to tell them that never once during the whole of my life did I write another poem.

Without knowing my Uncle Nandor, you don't know what it means to be rich. I don't mean those who are born into wealth (since money, like musical talent or early baldness, tends to run in families), or those who get hit by it in the prime of their lives. Uncle Nandor made money. He made it in a bank.

In my early childhood this seemed to me a more sensible thing to do than standing in a shop all day, as my father did. I had no idea how money was made because I'd never been in a bank. As far as I can remember there weren't many banks in Budapest in the thirties. People didn't have bank accounts or cheque books, or even money, come to think of it.

Uncle Nandor was a bank manager or, as it was called at the time, a bank director. 'Mr Bank Director Sir' was how he was addressed by everyone from the clerk at the post office to the janitor of the house where his apartment covered half of the first floor. It was magnificently furnished with armchairs and carved sideboards, and a glass case with china figurines which nobody was allowed to take out. I was particularly impressed by the two Pierrot dolls which sat dangling their legs on the sofa and a Negro pageboy made of wood who kept offering an ashtray in his outstretched hands. They were, however, only there to be admired and I was not allowed to touch them.

But I digress. A chronicler should begin with the subject's origin and family background. I should put on record that Nandor was the son of a poor back street tailor, even if it's unnecessary to say so. All composers, film directors or financial geniuses of the time were born in the overcrowded tenement flats of the big cities. Some were so poor that they couldn't even afford a christening and remained Jewish for the rest of their lives.

I never knew much about Uncle Nandor's early life. Childhood did not come into fashion until later. At the time it had only been noted for its nuisance value and my parents and aunts seldom talked about it. The only fact recorded by his sisters was that Nandor did badly in school.

'Your grandfather was furious,' my mother would recall with a beatific smile on her face. 'He pulled him out from under the bed where he was hiding and gave him a terrific beating with his leather belt. 'You – must – learn,' he shouted. And whack! the leather belt came down with every word.'

It was one of my mother's happier memories. She herself loved books, but who would spend money on a girl's education when there was not even money for her dowry? The family did not get out of poverty until Nandor's meteoric rise in the bank.

My grandfather's educational methods seem to have worked because Nandor took to banking like a young shark to water. After the death of my grandfather he moved to a different district and took his mother with him. Grandmother was a frail little woman who had always been afraid of her husband. Now she was afraid of Nandor, who would not allow her to keep in touch with her old cronies and supervised her every step. He paid fashionable doctors to cure her rheumatism and took her to elegant health resorts in Austria. They even went to the Salzburg festival to see Wagner's Götterdämmerung.

'Will this last much longer?' poor Grandmother had sighed after the first act, 'I'm suffering like a dog!'

Nandor would do anything for his family. He took a great interest in everyone's finances and somehow managed to make them dependent on him. It was his interest which caused such a terrific row between my parents when my father realised how much he had to pay on the loan which my mother had secured for him.

My father thoroughly disliked Uncle Nandor despite their being brothers-in-law. They were cousins as well which made them blood relations. 'Blood relations' was a fascinating term. It reminded me of the compact sealed with blood between Árpád and his seven chieftains after their arrival on the Great Hungarian Plain. Nevertheless, father and Nandor were not on speaking terms.

This was why he wasn't with us on the hot Sunday afternoon when my mother and I went to Hajós Street in Budapest for a family visit. I don't remember the occasion, only that, despite the heat, I had to wear my gloves and the black patent leather shoes which never got used to the shape of my feet. My mother must have been too hot in her heavy plum-coloured silk dress and the nearly new silver fox around her shoulders. We had to run to catch the number 42 streetcar and she was cross.

'Don't forget to curtsey when we arrive and say "please" and "thank you" when people talk to you, or they'll think that you're allowed to run wild. You've been picking up dreadful habits in school. I don't want to be ashamed of you!'

The dinner was splendid as always. The table was laid with embroidered linen and each napkin was folded in the shape of a fan. I had to sit up straight and not fiddle with them while the maid brought in the soup with thimble dumplings. It had a heavenly smell. I was hardly listening to the conversation around me as I watched Grandmother ladle out the soup, carefully avoiding the liver. Chicken liver was a great delicacy and I knew that she was saving it for me.

The soup was followed by stuffed veal in a cream sauce and the conversation around the table became even livelier. I tried to listen, but it was the same boring thing again about the man Hitler who'd come to power in Germany. I was more interested in Uncle Nandor who looked as if he wanted to make a speech.

'Don't talk to me about gratitude,' he declared to nobody in particular, although we hadn't. 'Do you remember József, the janitor in Liszt Ferenc Street?'

He waited until he had everyone's attention. We finished with the veal and Grandmother began to collect the plates. I was waiting for the crowning glory of the meal: chestnut cake with chocolate topping.

'Last year József came to see me and asked if I could give his son a job in the bank. You know the boy, he was born with one arm and naturally nobody would employ him. József begged me to help. The boy was miserable at home. They had no money. He was ever such a good lad. You know what these people are like.'

'I remember József,' my aunt said, 'He was a nice man. He used to hide me in their kitchen when you were chasing me.'

Uncle Nandor was not to be side-tracked. 'I'm not talking about him, but his son. You know I can never resist a good deed. Besides, he wouldn't expect to be paid proper rates so I arranged for him to be taken on as an errand boy.'

'Nandor has a heart of gold,' said Grandmother, who wasn't really listening. She started to cut the cake which diverted everyone's attention. After a few minutes my mother turned towards him.

'So what about József's son? Were they satisfied with him?'

'Oh yes,' Uncle Nandor said. 'Everybody liked him. Somebody suggested that the bank should get him a wooden arm. They found some orthopaedic firm which fitted an arm of exactly the right size. The boy was over the moon. I couldn't believe it when…' He stopped and looked around the table.

'He lost his other arm,' suggested my mother helpfully. Uncle Nandor gave her an annihilating look.

'We found out that that he stole ten pengoes from the till!' he declared, pointing at my mother with his fork. 'He stole from the bank which fed him! Naturally I had him dismissed at once. I told him to remove his artificial arm and go.'

He put a piece of the chestnut cake on his fork and frowned as if he were wondering what to do with a made-to-measure wooden arm.

2

What do I really know about Nandor, Grandmother, and my own mother, whom I can only see with a child's eye? I try to reconstruct them from faded photographs and a few letters which survived the Holocaust and my emigration to England nearly half a century ago. Their world has become submerged in the past, like Atlantis, and they have taken my childhood with them.

Was he really so rich? I am a hundred times as rich as he was. In my house there are as many bedrooms as people living in it (two, actually) and the hot water runs from the tap without a maid having to carry firewood to the boiler. There is a radio in my car which does not have to trail a wire behind when I drive, and I have a telephone in my pocket which works on belief. I have my own cinema in a box in the living room with five different programmes from which to choose. When Uncle Nandor went to a hotel, the commissioner opened the door for him but when I approach a supermarket the door opens for me on its own. You only have to live long enough to get the upper hand.

I was five years old when my sister Marinka got married. I didn't quite take in that she would leave home, only that she would take away the white table and chairs from our shared room. I was desperate. I ran from pillar to post insisting that the furniture should remain, but the grown-ups were deaf and dumb as usual.

Marinka was probably the most important person in my life, the source of my security, the object of my infantile adoration. My anxious mother was always busy with my father's customers so that it was Marinka who released me from the potty when she got home.

'My heart went out to you,' she later recalled, 'alone in the room, reaching up your arms to me to be rescued.' By this time, I was old enough to walk away from the potty but did not dare. The taboos and prohibitions connected with elimination loomed large over the childhood of my generation.

Marinka's engagement party took place in our dining room which had a window onto the street and was full of stuffed upholstery and heavy, carved furniture. She and my mother talked feverishly about tablecloths and cutlery and what to wear. I couldn't believe my ears when I was told that children (that meant me) were not allowed to take part in the celebrations.

What followed is as clear in my memory as the happy ending of a favourite film. Before the guests arrived, I was put into my parents' big double bed in the next room, sobbing and protesting, and told to go to sleep. It was the cruelest of rejections; it was expulsion from Paradise. I was so sick with envy and frustration that I couldn't even sob myself to sleep.

To get to the kitchen, people had to cross the room. When someone opened the door I could hear laughter and animated conversation, which increased my misery. Then the door opened again and Marinka came to the bed to see if I was asleep.

I grabbed at her sleeve. 'Don't go back!' I begged. 'Please stay with me! Don't go back, please, please, stay with me at least until I fall asleep!'

She said that it was impossible, but I kept begging her until she could no longer resist. She sat on the bed holding my hand and stayed with me until I fell asleep. The laughter and conversation next door went on without her. I clearly remember her looking anxiously at the dining room door but she remained, holding my hand in defiance of the guests. I was no longer the rejected one banished into darkness. My victory left me with a lifelong conviction that if I really, but really, wanted anything from my sister, I could get it. The pact between us didn't need to be tested; it was enough that it existed.

She is dead now, but as long as she lived there was no-one as close to me as she. We met or talked on the telephone three or four times a week, and later, when I was stranded in Vienna as a refugee for two years, we wrote long letters to each other. She stood by me during the upheavals of my life, and I followed her into emigration as if tied to her by an invisible cord.

I was nine years old when her daughter, Evi, was born. They lived not far from us, and I saw her all the time but, incredibly, I had no idea she was pregnant. I still don't understand how I managed this, since it must have been what she and my mother talked about all the time, and I must have seen newly bought layettes and baby clothes, yet on the day when I arrived home from school and my radiant mother embraced me, 'Congratulations! You have become an aunt!,' I was totally taken aback. 'Marinka has a baby girl!' she explained, but I didn't believe her. This must be the usual nonsense adults were telling me all the time. Even the nappies hanging on a line in the yard must have been part of some elaborate hoax that she and my sister had prepared for me.

The period of her pregnancy coincided with my relentless efforts to find out how babies were born. I pestered every adult from Tereza to Aunt Helen, begging them to tell me how it happened but my desperate questioning was only met by embarrassed giggles or a stern rebuke. 'When you get older you'll find out,' they said, or 'A good girl doesn't think about such things.' But I didn't want to be a good girl. I hated all adults and became angry and difficult. Neither the frequent slaps on my face, nor my mother's helpless puzzlement, changed the fact that I had become unmanageable. Nobody understood what had happened to me.

Evi was the darling of the family, but I was nine years older and, therefore, nine years wiser and nine years more knowledgeable than she. Once, when she was four or five she told me wistfully that in nine years' time we would be the same age, but I knew better. I explained to her things as I discovered them, like the meaning of the words 'symbol' and 'atheism' and that Adam and Eve had never existed. I was a teenager while she was still a child. It was, therefore, natural that it was I who became her mother's *confidante,* closer to her than anyone else. Now I can hardly believe that I never asked myself how Evi felt about all this. We live by the questions we refuse to ask ourselves.

Was it coincidence that Marinka often referred to a passage in her favourite book, *Josef and his Brothers,* by Thomas Mann? It was the story of the Biblical Joseph, his father's beautiful favourite, who was thrown into an empty well by his brothers. Joseph, who had always thought his brothers were equally pleased that their father preferred *him*, pondered in agony on what he'd done to infuriate his brothers. He finally understood that the unforgivable sin was to assume that they loved him more than they loved themselves.

According to Marinka, her husband was a tyrant whose violent outbursts she had to tolerate mainly for her daughter's sake. I listened to her with angry sympathy and expected her to divorce him as soon as circumstances allowed. But the circumstances were never right. I was too young to understand that it was not divorce either of them wanted, but to force the other to admit that they were right. To the best of my knowledge, neither of them was ever unfaithful; and, on the one occasion when Dani briefly eyed another woman, Marinka was distraught. For half a century they were never apart. The frustration which kept them together for a lifetime was indistinguishable from love. When Dani died, I expected my sister to give a sigh of relief. I was taken aback when, at his funeral, she treated me like a stranger. How was I, my sister's faithful confidante, to know that the opposite of love is not hate, but indifference? During the whole of her married life, she unloaded her grievances on me and I listened and commiserated with her. Dani must have felt that I was the instigator of their rows, because he couldn't stand me, and for decades I was supposed to go to their home only in his absence. His resentment had become a fact of life which I accepted without trying to understand. As I have said, we live by the questions which we fail to ask ourselves.

Marinka died in her early eighties. After her funeral, I returned to her empty house. As I walked distraughtly up and down in her bedroom, I noticed a photo album on the dressing table, which I had never seen before. I picked it up and began idly to turn the pages.There were old fashioned studio photos of our parents standing stiffly in front of an ornate table; wedding photos of her and Dani; my sister with Evi as a baby, as well as innumerable snapshots and formal photographs. Evi's wedding, Evi's graduation ceremony, Evi on the beach, Evi with her son, Evi with her son's family. She was the daughter, of course, but where was I? I shook the album in case a photo had become stuck between the pages, but there were none of me.

The scene at her engagement which I so vividly remembered all my life could, of course, never have happened. Even if Marinka had wanted to stay with me, it would have been impossible. Someone would have fetched her. It was one of those early memories which we create later in life, superimposing fragments of real events on each other until they become events which *ought to have* happened.

3

The Hungarian version of 'once upon a time' contains an element of doubt which is difficult to translate. The nearest to the original would probably be: 'Once upon a time there was or there wasn't.' Either there was or there wasn't a King who had two daughters. One was sixteen years older than the other who was the apple of her father's eye. One day the King mounted his white stallion and said to his elder daughter, 'Take care of the little one because I might never return.'

There was nobody else in the room as I watched my father shaving in front of the wardrobe mirror. He stirred the water in a bowl with swift movements to make lather like whipped cream and put it on his face. I loved watching him transforming himself into a clown and then becoming my father again. He took the razor from its sheath and began to scrape the lather off his cheek, holding his nose with two fingers and pursing his mouth, which made me giggle. He grinned at me. I smiled back but he didn't respond, and I realized that what I took for a grin was merely a grimace into the mirror.

My father could whistle beautifully, repeating tunes on first hearing. According to the little information I'd picked up over the years, Grandmother Forster feared and mistrusted his musical ability. Once, when he was a child, the teacher brought him home personally to tell his parents that he had a good ear and offered to give him piano lessons. Grandmother did not want to hear of it. In the village where she came from musicians were not of high standing. A man should be making money instead of tinkering with musical instruments.

Either it was true or it wasn't… My strong Grandmother Forster must have beaten the resistance out of him early in his life because he never learned to play music. When Marinka became a young girl, my mother managed somehow to acquire an upright piano and she underwent, as I did later, the ritual torture of piano lessons. She too was tone deaf and hated practising the scales. My father, who was about forty at the time, tried to teach himself to play but gave it up in the face of the family's resistance for whom this proved only that he didn't care about the shop and that my mother would starve in her old age.

He hadn't returned from the concentration camp after the war. This is how we used to say it: 'hasn't returned.' For years after the war people would say: 'My son hasn't returned from Russia' or 'My sister hasn't returned from Auschwitz' as if there was uncertainty about their fate.

My father has no grave. It was only much later that I started to dream that I was in a streetcar on my way to visit him. Suddenly it struck me that I hadn't seen him for years, even decades. How could I have been so neglectful? There must be a reason. Is he dead? In the dream, I desperately try to recall where his grave is, but I can't place it anywhere. But if he has no grave, he cannot be dead. He must have been waiting for me all these years in St Lőrinc but I never went to see him. Cringing with guilt and shame I always wake up before the streetcar reaches its destination.

4

School begins at the age of six in Hungary. I was six when we moved from Márton Street to St Lőrinc, a dusty village near Budapest. I don't know whose idea it was that my father should start a business there. With the help of a bank loan which Uncle Nandor had secured for him, he had a house built with an adjacent shop to be run by himself and my mother.

The shop sold straw for litter and hay and corn fodder for domestic animals. For about a year my parents had a shop assistant called Mr. Kovács who asked me trick questions and taught my father to ride a bicycle but he had to go because they couldn't afford his salary. Many years later, when Hungary became a 'People's Democracy' under Stalin, I learned that Mr. Kovács had been the workforce whom my capitalist father had exploited, and that, therefore, I couldn't become a member of the Communist Party. For this I owe him eternal gratitude.

The newly built house in St Lőrinc consisted of two rooms and space for a future bathroom into which my mother hoped eventually to install running water. We had a separate kitchen in a lean-to and there was some talk about an indoor toilet. In the meantime water had to be fetched by old Terez whom my mother employed as cook, maid, and substitute German governess in the hope that I would pick up some German from her. Terez belonged to a small ethnic minority with a terrible German dialect but preferred to talk in broken Hungarian.'My legs do me pain,' she used to chant, 'Ach, my legs do me pain.' She repeated it again and again like a broken gramophone until everyone stopped hearing it.

It was only half a century later that nursing my aching legs I suddenly realized that Terez was in pain. It's no use complaining to the young; they're hard of hearing.

The new Elementary School at St Lőrinc had two entrances, one for the girls, the other for the boys. With a little help from my mother I managed to read the number **1930** on the wall which thrilled me because it was the year in which I started school. It turned out, however, to simply commemorate the year in which the school was built.

I was the only Jewish child in the school. I understood that 'Jewish' meant that we were better off than the others. I would invite children to play hide and seek among the bales of straw at the back of the shop and we would climb into the forbidden hay loft. The air in the shop was thick with dust so that the till was in a little office in a glass cubicle near the entrance door. Sometimes, I was allowed to sit by the till and became the princess in a glass tower, watching the customers buying fodder for the horse or corn for the chicken.

My best friend was called Daisy. She had no father and her mother probably gave her such an exotic name to compensate for it. Every Mariska and Piroska in the class wanted to be friends with her, but it was with me that she walked home from school, swinging our arms to show we were friends.

At home, we would sneak into our front room which was seldom used. The shutters were always down to protect the furniture from sunlight and this gave the room a mysterious gloom. There was a dining table with carved legs, six chairs upholstered in red velvet, a glass show case with china ornaments, and a dresser with two Sabbath candlesticks on it. We could barely discern their silver splendour in the light which slanted through the slabs of the shutter and lit up the dancing dust particles in the air. The room smelt of mothballs and wax which, Daisy said in a whisper, was like the smell of incense in the church.

I would tiptoe to the glass cabinet and take out, piece by piece, the cups and saucers of my mother's bone china coffee set which I was forbidden to touch. I would hand them to Daisy who rubbed them against her cheek before she gave them back. She said that she too would like to be Jewish but there was nothing we could do about it.

We didn't mix with the boys at school. Boys shouted and fought – which was why angels and fairies were always portrayed as girls, while imps and devils were always boys. (To tell the truth, my mother once found me in the hayloft with a boy and there was a terrible row. But I've completely forgotten what we did and, in any case, that was a year or two later). Girls wearing trousers were a scandal and when a girl tried to whistle like a boy, St Mary in heaven burst into tears.

I knew this from Daisy who was a Catholic and regularly reported to me what the Virgin thought. She wore a cross on a silver chain around her neck which was to save her from disaster, such as being eaten by a wild animal, or falling over a precipice. However poor her mother was, Daisy had a Christmas tree every year. I was usually invited on Boxing Day to pluck from it the Christmas candy wrapped in silver and gold. Daisy maintained that the tree was brought during the night by Little Jesus, which no one of our age should any longer believe, but I let it pass.

It was a stormy friendship. Once we fell out because Daisy said that the Jews had crucified Jesus. I checked it at home and told her that it was a wicked lie because it was the Romans who did it, not the Jews. But we soon made up because we had a passion which was not shared by anybody else.

It was the love of Art. Daisy and I were collectors of shiny embossed pictures sold in series by news agents and tobacconists. They represented flowers and animals, but the most valuable ones were sold on their own. One could swap two exotic birds for an angel peeping out from behind a cloud. Two pixies were worth a lady with blonde or black tresses cascading down to her knees. We glued the pictures into albums and discussed them with the rapture of connoisseurs. However, I couldn't keep up with Daisy who went to Sunday School where you could get holy pictures for good behaviour.

'I'll give you my hussar on a horse for St Theresa,' I offered, but Daisy wouldn't have it.

'I can't swap a saint. It would be a sin. But if you give me the hussar I'll let you come with me to the church.'

I'd had a fleeting glimpse of the interior of the Catholic church before, but I'd never had the opportunity to look around properly.

'You know I'm not supposed to go there,' I protested feebly.

'You can tell your Mum that we went to see my Granny. It'll only be a white lie and we could pray for forgiveness while we are there,' Daisy argued, 'If you also give me the angel in the blue robe, I'll pray for you.'

My heart was pounding with excitement and the sense of wrongdoing as we crossed the porch of the church. Daisy genuflected and crossed herself which I tried to imitate, then quickly looked around hoping that no-one had seen me. The interior was almost dark after the glaring afternoon sunshine. It took me some time to get used to the twilight, made even more mysterious by dozens of flickering candles in front of paintings and statues. The wax statues were like real people, only more so. Real ladies could never have such golden hair and milky complexions, real men could never have their beards in such symmetrical curls. I was overwhelmed with admiration and felt my skin tingle. I was particularly taken with a painting of St Elisabeth of Hungary on a white horse, distributing food to the poor. She was defying the orders of her wicked husband who could be seen lurking behind a tree. The painter had caught her at the very moment when the food miraculously changed into roses so that her husband could not punish her. The poor at the roadside looked rather crestfallen but St Elisabeth turned her face towards heaven and smiled.

Daisy was praying before the altar and I felt that it wouldn't be polite not to do the same. I put my palms together to recite my evening prayer asking God to watch over me in my sleep and reunite me with my family in the morning. It did not make much sense under the circumstances but the only other prayer I knew was in Hebrew, which I somehow felt was inappropriate.

Hebrew was a language which nobody understood unless they were Jewish. It was God's personal language in which he had talked to Adam and Eve and dictated the Ten Commandments to Moses. I was proud that we had a shared language with God, even though I didn't understand a word of it. Neither, apparently, did anyone else I knew, apart from the rabbi. Hebrew was probably the reason why He brought us out from Egypt (or I wouldn't be in St Lőrinc) and made us His chosen people.

Suddenly I remembered that God was everywhere and could see everything. Could He even be present in a Catholic church? If so, He'd know that I was committing a Sin.

The light from the tinted windows slanted across the nave and ended up in coloured pools on the floor. It was similar to the Cave of the Dragon in the amusement park where my father had once taken me. The cave could be entered only by a chain of open wagons pulled by a dragon with blinking red eyes. His nose blew sparks in the dark and some of the children screamed. Suddenly the light came on as if by magic to illuminate a recess in the wall and there was Snow White and the Seven Dwarfs. Snow White was smiling and turning her head while the dwarfs hammered rhythmically on a rock. We could hardly take in its splendour when the dragon continued its journey in the dark, until the next recess where the castle of the Sleeping Beauty could be seen with the whole household asleep.

Then came Cinderella and her wicked sisters. When it was over I jumped out from the wagon and ran to my father in a daze.

The interior of the Catholic church was an even greater aesthetic experience. St Elisabeth's blue gown was more beautiful than the satin frock of Snow White and the colorful pools of light on the ground more thrilling than the red sparks in the dragon's cave. I was overwhelmed by Beauty. The word 'kitsch' did not enter into my vocabulary until much later.

5

Being a Jewish child had potential advantages. 'The boys ganged up and called me names because of my red hair,' I explained my torn socks and dirty pinafore to my mother one day, omitting the fact that I kicked the gang leader in the shin and shopped the rest to the teacher.

It was a molehill rapidly taking on the proportion of the Himalayas. 'They had been calling the poor child a redheaded Jew,' my sister reported to my aunt who told it to Uncle Nandor. I didn't realise that I was onto a good thing until the next Sunday afternoon when we went to see my grandmother in Budapest. By then the whole family was alerted to my martyrdom and vied with each other as to who could spoil me the most. If an extra dollop of whipped cream was the reward for defenders of the faith, I had no objection to being one.

Then, I caught typhoid fever for which there was no cure at the time. The doctor had a red note pinned on the door warning that nobody should enter the house.

Hospital, even if there was one in St Lőrinc, was not even considered. My bed was moved into the front room, with a cot for my mother next to it. I vaguely remember a uniformed nurse who came to help her, but I screamed when she came near me. It was my mother who put me into cold compresses and sat up with me during the night. Neither my father, nor Marinka (who had a five month old baby) were allowed to come near me for weeks. My mother was a virtual prisoner even after the fever subsided and it looked as if I would survive. She had put on weight in St Lőrinc and was fighting a hopeless battle with her appetite. At mealtimes, she refused to eat but would later sneak into the kitchen and stuff herself with the remnants of the meal. During my illness she would sit by my bed trying to make me swallow some thin gruel (I was only allowed liquid or sieved food) but when she thought that I was asleep she would furtively finish the meal, using the same spoon with which she was feeding me.

When I was on my feet again and the quarantine was over, my mother and I went to visit Grandmother and Aunt Helen in Budapest. These visits had usually been a treat but on that particular afternoon I was very cross and made myself as unpleasant as I could. The family was supposed to have gathered at Grandmother's to see me after my recovery from the typhoid fever, yet all they wanted to do was talk to my mother.

I went to the kitchen in search of the maid. 'Have you heard that I've been hovering between life and death and that my parents nearly lost me?' I asked her importantly, but she was about to leave for her Sunday outing and shooed me back to the dining room.

'Can we go home now?' I asked my mother loudly to embarrass her. To my surprise, she agreed.

'We really must go,' she said, 'The weather is terrible and it will be ages before we get home.'

Grandmother protested while she came with us to the hall to get our coats. Kisses were given and promises made, gloves were hunted for and found, a scarf was borrowed and a slice of cake was wrapped in tissue paper for the journey. At last we were in the street and my mother pulled me under her umbrella.

'Can't you walk faster? We'll be soaked before we get to the tram.'

Not a word about my behaviour, no comments on my manners. Later I would remember that she was flushed and breathless, but at the time I didn't care. We must have missed the No. 42 tram because the shelter was empty. Despite my protestation, Mother unwound her scarf and tied it around my neck and I sulked. We sat in silence until the yellow lamps of the approaching tram emerged from the mist. It was the terminus and we had to wait for the conductor to smoke a cigarette before he allowed us to board.

'This is better,' my mother sighed, 'Do you want your book?'

The light was too dim for reading. I knelt on the seat to watch the raindrops on the window chasing each other without ever winning the race. The tram rattled along Üllői Avenue towards the suburb of Kispest where the houses were smaller and the distance between them was greater. Eventually I got bored. Using my mother's scarf as a pillow, I curled up on the bench and fell asleep.

I was woken by my mother trying to remove her scarf from under my head. I sat up and saw that she had a nosebleed. Her handkerchief was soaked in blood.

'I didn't want to wake you but I have no more hankies,' she apologised, 'Move away a bit, will you?' She leaned back, holding the scarf to her nose and put her feet up on the seat. Her hairpins had fallen out and her petticoat was showing. I'd never seen her like this and knew that something was very wrong. Luckily the carriage was almost empty but for two men talking in the rear and the guard who was walking from one end of the tram to the other. Presently he stopped by us.

'Bend your head a bit more,' he advised my mother. 'Pinch your nose and take a deep breath.' I watched helplessly as the scarf became saturated with blood, but there was nothing else to hold to her nose. In distress, she went to the outer platform to remove her linen petticoat.

The tram had left the suburb of Kispest for the open country, swaying a little in the wind. Left and right of the track there was nothing but muddy fields. It was dark outside, and the rain hammered relentlessly on the window.

My anxiety grew by the minute. What did she think, letting strangers to see her so dishevelled? Blood was spreading on the petticoat which she held to her nose, like ink on blotting paper. I was too embarrassed to look around. It seemed an eternity since we had got on the tram. Couldn't she do something? She did not speak, but leaned back on the seat with eyes closed. I would probably have been less alarmed had I ever seen her ill, but my mother had never had so much as a cold. The tram seemed to move like a snail.

At last, we were home and the grown-ups took over. Everything was well again. Next day, however, she did not get up and the doctor was sent for. I knew him well because he used to come to the house daily while I had typhoid. He greeted me with some jocular remark but I was in a hurry to leave. It was a God-sent opportunity to spend the day with my sister and her baby daughter who lived at the other end of St Lőrinc. If I was lucky Mother wouldn't stop me tomorrow either.

It was strange to see my mother in bed and my father so worried. On Wednesday morning, the doctor said that it couldn't be typhoid because the incubation period was over, but by the evening the symptoms were unmistakable. On Thursday afternoon, my Aunt Helen and Uncle Nandor arrived from Budapest in a taxi, followed by my sister, Marinka, and her husband. Aunt Helen and Uncle Nandor brought with them a professor of medicine from Budapest. He went into the room to join our doctor while the rest of us stood huddled together on the landing. After a while he came out drying his hands on a towel. He was in his shirtsleeves and looked worried.

'We can't stop the haemorrhage. We need a blood transfusion,' he said, 'Could any of you…'

My brother-in-law was removing his jacket and turning up his sleeve as he followed the doctor into the room. My sister was nowhere to be seen. I went out into the dark courtyard to look for her. She was at the bottom of the yard, walking up and down. 'Please God, don't let her die. Shema yisrael, adonai elohenu. She mustn't die. Lord, let her recover…' When she saw me she grabbed my arm. 'Stay with me,' she said. I didn't like being dragged like this. An unspeakable horror was descending on us but I wriggled free. I went to the kitchen to Terez

'When are we going to have dinner?' I asked.

Then it was night and I was in a taxi with my aunt and uncle and the doctor, going to Budapest. I loved being in a taxi but Aunt Helen was sobbing loudly and the men looked grim which something in me refused to understand. 'I've learned a prayer in the school. Shall I recite it?' I said brightly to my uncle, ready to show off. 'Hush,' said my aunt, embracing me, 'It is late. Shut your eyes and try to sleep. Count silently up to a hundred.'

'That's nothing. I can count to a thousand easily,' I retorted.

6

Shortly after my mother's death they put me in a boarding school. I did not want to go. I fought it tooth and nail and kicked up a fuss when my aunt took me there. The headmistress thought that I would settle in more easily if I didn't have any visitors for a while.

Mrs. Malnai's boarding school was expensive, and claimed to be progressive.

'This is the new girl whose Mummy had just died. We must all be very kind to her,' a teacher introduced me, but the boarders looked at me with suspicion. I was different from them. I knew nothing about the pecking order in the queue for breakfast, or about choosing partners in the crocodile, or that one had to drink one's fill from tooth mugs in the bathroom since water with meals was forbidden, on the grounds that it took away our appetite. Like any tribe governed by dictators, the boarders pretended to live by the laws of the adults, while following their own. In St Lőrinc I could have coped, but children in the Malnai were a different breed from those in the village school. They had had holidays abroad and had been to the opera and seen theatre performances. They knew more than I did on every subject. I became hapless and distraught, like an alien chick in the farmyard.

Shortly after my arrival I found large tufts of hair in my comb and realized, in horror, that my hair was falling out. The doctor said that losing one's hair was usual after typhoid fever. It would grow back and it was nothing to be ashamed of.

Nothing to be ashamed of! Within a short time I was totally bald. To my horror I began to wet the bed, which put me beyond the pale. The whole dormitory watched with righteous indignation and unconcealed glee the ritual of my sheets being changed in the morning. I begged in vain for my aunt and uncle to take me away. My father was no help. I seldom saw him because he was in a dispute with my mother's family about the house, and was no longer on speaking terms with them.

I remember sitting at my bench at the back of the classroom with the windows open so that I could see the top of a poplar bowing in the wind. It would have been nice to watch it but the class was taking dictation, and I had to keep up.

Suddenly the tip of my pencil broke. 'Have you got a spare pencil?' I whispered to the girl next to me, but she shook her head and went on writing.

'I need a pencil sharpener! Can you lend me one?'

'Stop nudging me,' she whispered and pulled away. I looked around in alarm. 'A pencil! Have you got a pencil? Please! Have you got one?' The girl to her right further up picked up her pencil case and deliberately put it in her desk. The others sniggered. The teacher on her dais went on dictating in a drowsy voice. I missed what she had said and began to panic. I tugged at the sleeve of the girl in front of me. She turned round and stared at me. I must have been a spectacle, red in the face and sweating as I mimed sharpening a pencil with my hands. She stared at me and returned to her writing.

The teacher continued dictating. She would never stop now to give me a break. The sentences of the dictation followed each other relentlessly, like the coaches of a departing train, and every second diminished my hope of catching them.

'Please give me another pencil!' I begged again, but they bent over their books with conspicuous diligence. I could no longer hold on to the words which rolled by, to be lost for ever. I could no longer keep them in my mind; they disappeared and were beyond retrieval.

I began to sob and gasp for air. When the teacher stopped dictating at last and stepped down from her dais to ask me what had happened, I couldn't explain. I was beside myself and had to be taken to the sick bay.

Orphans were supposed to be sad, but I didn't feel sad at all. When I pinched my arm very hard I managed to produce a few drops of tears but that was not the same as being able to sob with grief. I looked into the mirror and said: 'She's a poor orphan girl who will never see her mother again,' which only made me giggle. Yet I knew that my mother had caught the typhoid from me because I wouldn't let anybody else wash me or give me my medicine. I was a wicked, unfeeling child who had killed her mother and did not even cry for her. I wanted to die. I tried to cut my wrist with a table knife, crisscrossing it without reaching the artery but I still didn't feel any sadness. I didn't know how to mourn.

My life as a boarder in the Malnai felt like an eternity, but in reality it lasted less than a school year. The reason I could not stay at Hajós Street was that Grandmother was ill, and Aunt Helen had tried to keep my mother's death from her. Poor Grandmother was tied into a cobweb of kind lies about the whereabouts of my mother, and they couldn't risk allowing her to see me. When she died, I moved to live with Aunt Helen and her husband Marci in their apartment, which occupied half the first floor of the house. The other half was where Uncle Nandor lived.

7

Someone (probably Oscar Wilde) said that there was no hatred on earth like the hatred of a well-brought up young girl for her mother. There must be some truth in this, since being relentlessly monitored is like being a prisoner.

'A diamond has to be shaped, a young tree has to be pruned,' Aunt Helen, who liked received wisdom, would declare. But she must have been good to me, otherwise I couldn't have felt safe enough to lock myself in the bathroom, fervently wishing her dead. It didn't help that I knew that I ought to be grateful. Had I stayed with my disengaged father in the wilderness of St Lőrinc I could never have gone to a grammar school and my life would have taken a different turn.

Dust to dust, ashes to ashes, she is nothing now but a shadow remembered by no-one else but me. Does it matter whether she was responsible for the misery of my adolescence? But it matters tremendously to me, because I want to know if I deserve to burn in hell for having pretended that I had no choice but to leave her behind when I came to England. She was old, ill and lonely. If self deception leads us to hell, blue upholstered heaven must be empty all the time.

The memory of my painful and chaotic adolescence is full of holes. The years of growing up seem to have melted into each other. I have hardly any recollection of Aunt Helen's husband, Uncle Marci, with whom I lived for eight long years; neither do I remember how I changed from star pupil in the elementary school into a near-failure in the secondary.

Every day I performed complicated jumps over the cobblestones on the way to school without discovering that doing my homework would have helped. I regularly misplaced my books, forgot to consult the timetable, took the wrong books with me, and walked to school every morning hoping for a miracle. My friends, whom I regularly exercised in the virtue of tolerance, let me crib their homework and covered up for me, but they couldn't help me find my lost belongings. My thrifty aunt refused to believe that I wasn't callously indifferent towards my gloves, umbrellas, scarves, purses, books and pens, and treated their loss as deliberate defiance. It was agony to face her and confess to the latest disaster.

I was about thirteen or fourteen when I met Agnes Ipper and learned about the necessity of random kindness to strangers. This was in the late 1930's when the law restricting the employment of Jewish teachers already existed, so that she couldn't get a job in a state school. Like most teachers who were Jewish in terms of the fascist laws, she gave private lessons in her home. My friends talked enthusiastically about her weekly seminars on music and literature for teenage girls whom she introduced to Baudelaire and Rilke and made them read her favorites Jacobsen and Selma Lagerlöf. Those in the class who attended the 'culture group' said she was wonderful, a world apart from the teachers in the school who had to be curtsied to and called Ma'am.

I begged Aunt Helen to let me join them. She didn't think much of wasting money but I persuaded her that Culture, although not part of the school curriculum, would improve my school reports. Finally she agreed and I made an appointment to introduce myself to Mrs Ipper.

I ran up the four flights of stairs to her flat, full of anticipation, only to realise that I was too early. I turned down the top of my glove to see the time, but my watch was not on my wrist. I began to hunt through my pockets, although I was sure that I hadn't put it there. I squatted on the landing and shook out the contents of my satchel, praying for a miracle. I ran downstairs and then back up, well aware that I wouldn't find it.

I had lost it, lost the watch, the expensive birthday present wristwatch. The nauseous truth was only too familiar. However often it happened, the absence of something which had been there shook me to the core. I've lost it. The horror that something which **IS** can become something which **IS NOT** was almost more than I could bear.

'They'll kill me at home,' I sobbed when Agnes Ipper opened the door. She must have seen me from the kitchen window and came out to help me collect the scattered contents of my satchel.

'Now sit down and tell me what happened.'

'I can't find my watch and my aunt will kill me.'

'She is your mother's sister, isn't she? The girls told me that you'd lost your mother and that your father lives elsewhere.'

'In St Lőrinc. I don't see him very often because I'm living with my aunt,' I said inconsequentially. 'It's not that. It's that I'm always losing things and Aunt Helen says she's at the end of her tether. She doesn't believe that I don't do it on purpose.' Agnes gave me a handkerchief and sat down facing me. She listened patiently to what I told her between my sniffs and hiccups.

'How can I pull myself together if I can't?' I sobbed. 'My aunt will say that I lost it on purpose, to spite her. What's wrong with me? I've tried to kill myself but I couldn't do it.'

'Couldn't do what?'

'I stepped off the pavement deliberately to be killed by a car, but it stopped. The driver managed to brake.'

'How dreadful! Poor man!'

Adults could only think of themselves. The driver was the same. When he jumped out of the car and I told him that I wanted to die, he shouted: 'And what about me?'

Agnes was tall and strong with an abundance of brown hair and I thought her beautiful. She asked what books I was reading and if I'd ever been to a concert. I told her everything about myself although I didn't expect to live to join the 'culture group' after Aunt Helen had noticed the loss of the watch. After a while she told me that it was time for me to go and I stood up.

She hesitated. 'Try not to be found out until tomorrow,' she said. 'I'll meet you after school and buy you another watch.'

I believed her even though watches were expensive and I knew that she had little money. There was, of course, no question of my ever paying her back. I was a stranger to her, yet next day she was there at the school gate and took me to a jeweller's shop. The new watch was so similar to the one I had lost that Aunt Helen never noticed the difference.

8

I have a photograph of my Aunt Helen as a teenager standing next to my beautiful mother who must have been in her twenties at the time; a thistle standing next to a rose. Aunt Helen had a squint and wore glasses. Her arranged marriage had ended in divorce, but their brother Nandor provided her with the dowry which she needed to marry again. The money enabled Uncle Marci to become owner of a large and prosperous chemist shop. Their lifestyle was way beyond what my mother could ever have hoped for.

Had she been jealous of my mother's beauty? Did my mother envy her fur coat and diamond ring? Aunt Helen would have been horrified if I had asked her. The order of things by which she lived did not allow such questions. Sisters and brothers, like parents and children, were bound to love one another, so that jealousy between sisters would have been unnatural. Questions like this would only distress her as another proof of my wayward thinking.

Aunt Helen spent her life tiptoeing around her husband with adoration and awe. Uncle Marci was the only one in the family who had been to university and his diploma, hand written on parchment and sealed with wax and red ribbon, hung in a frame on the wall, for everyone to see. Not many people did, since they had no friends to entertain. They never went out together, except for short walks round the block after dinner, which was good for the digestion. Two or three times a week, Uncle Marci would take his hat and stick, kiss Aunt Helen on the forehead, and go out to meet his friends and colleagues. It was understood that ladies were not invited to these meetings. Neither did Aunt Helen join him on the occasional Sunday afternoons when, elegantly dressed in spats and a butterfly tie, he went out for the rest of the day. 'You'll learn in time why women have big aprons.' Aunt Helen once said to me, 'It covers everything they don't want to see.'

Uncle Marci was a stocky man who walked like a soldier and kept himself trim on the skating rink and the tennis court. When I knew him he had no hair but wore his baldness with the same air of distinction as he did his butterfly ties and his cane with the silver handle. My mother used to call him a perfect gentleman because he kissed her hand and was always impeccably polite to his wife.

He would be still asleep in the morning when I got ready for school so that I had to be careful not to make any noise. Aunt Helen would already be fully dressed and her face made up by then, because no self respecting woman should be seen by her husband with her dress in disarray when he woke up. She was proud of the fact that Uncle Marci had never seen her in her underwear.

When I was little, on dark and cold winter mornings, Aunt Helen used to wake me with a kiss and put on my socks while I was still under the duvet. My school uniform was waiting for me on a chair, washed and ironed by the maid. Aunt Helen packed my sandwiches and checked whether my blouse was properly tucked into my skirt. She frequently went to the school to make inquiries about my progress and checked if I had done my homework. The battle between us began only when I reached puberty.

'You must have hurt yourself down below. Put your panties in the laundry basket and get a clean pair,' she said, turning away in embarrassment. The maid who witnessed the scene whispered something into her ear. 'Nonsense!' Aunt Helen retorted angrily, 'She's only a child!'

Eventually the problem got sorted out without anyone talking about it. In any case, information about such things came from one's friends. The Secret was the cause of endless rumours and speculations among us. My friend Annie once borrowed a book from the bookshelf of her uncle with the title 'Psychopathologia Sexualis' but if we hoped it would shed some light on what men and women did in bed we were sadly disappointed. It had disgusting pictures and descriptions of weird illnesses, but nothing about the Thing itself.

As I reached the higher grades I was probably the only one who didn't have a boyfriend. Aunt Helen didn't give birthday parties so I was seldom invited to parties where I could meet boys. My sporting activities were conducted under Aunt Helen's eyes. I was clumsy on the skating rink and the tennis coach swore I had two left hands. Most of my classmates were allowed to go on outings with boys and girls of their own age, and the lucky ones had brothers or cousins who escorted them whenever there was a dance. Aunt Helen thought that I should concentrate on my schoolwork instead.

I didn't even know what to say to a boy. But, oh God, if only there would be one to wait for me by the gate when we left school! The girls swarmed onto the street and their faces lit up when they saw their boyfriends. If only once, just once, a boy was waiting for me! All the girls would see me triumphantly linking my arm into his, and I would never ask for anything else in my life. I had wild fantasies about addressing an unknown young man in the street and begging him to meet me after school. Why not? They were human after all and there must be one who'd understand how desperate I was. I could tell him that he didn't have to see me ever again if he didn't want to. Naturally, it came to nothing. I would no sooner dare talk to an unknown young man on the street than fly to the moon.

Aunt Helen tried relentlessly to improve me. She took me to a nerve specialist for advice about my untidiness, to an orthopaedic surgeon because of my bad posture, and to a dermatologist to cure my adolescent spots. The orthopaedic surgeon suggested a canvas and whalebone corset with a steel collar around my neck to keep me erect, which made my life a misery until I refused to wear it. The dermatologist prescribed a liquid to be put on my face every morning which stretched my skin until it shone as if covered in oil.

'Wipe it off for God's sake,' said one of the teachers in disgust. As if I could! My face was shining like a full moon and would probably crack if I smiled. There was no point in protesting any louder than I did, because all these trials and tribulations were for my benefit. I knew I was clumsy and untidy, and had freckles on my face, and that Aunt Helen's strenuous efforts to improve me were justified. I didn't like myself either.

'Please don't forget that she needs shoulder pads because her shoulders are sloping,' she would say to the dressmaker, who knelt in front of me with pins in her mouth, 'You should lower the hem a little because she's knock-kneed. And no belt please, it would only emphasise that she has no waist.'

I didn't get a new dress very often, however, because the money was better spent on the embroidered sheets and pillow cases piling up in the wardrobe, to eventually become my trousseau. Everyday wear didn't have to be nice. I remember the tough canvas material which she said would make excellent underwear, and would last for years. When it was sewn up into a tubular shape with shoulder straps it was so stiff that it stood on the floor on its own. It did not do much for the shape of my developing bust but she was right; it proved impossible to wear out for years. A schoolgirl's appearance was of no consequence. Aunt Helen's efforts on my behalf would only reap their reward when, at eighteen, I would suddenly emerge as a young lady with flawless complexion and perfect poise.

9

The Maria Terézia Grammar school, where I started my eight years of secondary education in 1934, was a pompous old two storey building parading its yellow facade on the elegant Andrássy Avenue. Uncle Nandor had to pull strings (besides paying the fees) to get me in, because by that time the school was trying to limit its intake of Jewish pupils. There were seven or eight Jewish girls in the class. We lived in a different world from the gentile girls who attended sports clubs and dancing classes to which we would never be admitted. As far as I can remember, there was no overt hostility in the class but we didn't mix, and it was amongst ourselves that we made friends and foes. The teachers, I think, were reasonably fair. They must have been under pressure to keep the school records 'balanced', yet it would have been impossible not to give top marks to Kati Schulhof, who was best in maths, and to Vera Székely, whose retentive memory made exams child's play for her. It was only later that the distance between the Jewish and the Aryan girls became a gulf.

A rose was a rose was a rose even then, but an Aryan was not an Aryan unless he could prove that he was not Jewish. The Nuremberg law of 1934 stipulated that only persons whose four grandparents were of 'pure blood' could be registered as Aryans. Grandparents became a potential menace. A Jewish grandmother whose bones had fallen into dust long ago could ruin a career; two or more Jewish grandparents could be the cause of deportation and death. Even the best families were gripped by the fear of discovering a hitherto unknown Jewish ancestor. As if taking part in a hilarious farce, the whole of Europe queued in front of parish churches and registry offices. Thousands of aristocratic heads bent over parchment, yellowed with age, to scrutinise the family tree; hundreds of counterfeiters rubbed their hands before picking up the razor blade to erase great-grandfather's denomination from his birth certificate. Everyone, from the Baltic to the Mediterranean, was compelled to submit documentation about his or her racial origin. The only people who had no need to collect documents to prove their ancestry were, of course, the Jews.

By the time I was preparing for my final exams at the grammar school, it looked as if the fertile agricultural land of Hungary grew nothing but family trees. They were a source of rivalry among my Aryan classmates whose heads were full of ball-gowns and dashing young officers on leave from the front. The eight Jewish girls had no such preoccupations. Our young men had also been called up but they had to wear a yellow armband to show they had no weapons, and they had to do slave labour in Russia, behind the German and Hungarian lines.

We were not bothered with family trees. In any case, my family's coat of arms would probably have contained a rickety wheelbarrow in which my ancestors had pushed their goods across Europe. We didn't compete with our gentile classmates. We were lucky to be in the school at all.

Krisztina, whose mother was a countess, boasted to her friends that the origin of her family went back six centuries, but my friend Kati was unimpressed. 'Who cares if she's descended from Attila the Hun? I have exactly the same number of ancestors as she has,' she said scornfully, 'and they've probably been brighter than hers, in any case, according to the law of probability…'

'For heaven's sake, don't start on the law of probability,' I begged. 'You promised to help me with the maths assignment, though God knows why I'm bothering. I'll be an equally good factory worker without the final examination.' This was 1941. Hungary wasn't yet at war, but every week brought a further turn of the screw, restricting the life of the Jewish population. Many of my friends' fathers had lost their jobs and Uncle Marci's pharmacy was threatened by the law relating to the number of Jews allowed to work in a professional capacity. There were rumours of atrocities committed against the Jewish population in Poland and Germany, but they must have been exaggeration, so few people believed them. The hardest thing to come by was information. We had no access to foreign newspapers, and tuning in to foreign broadcasts was against the law. Those who had a radio that was good enough would risk listening to the BBC late at night, but no-one knew anything for sure.

My anxiety was not focused on world politics, however, but on my stockings. My only pair of silk stockings had been set aside for Thursday evenings when Aunt Helen escorted me to Bruno Petriss' dancing class. She would put on her silver fox and I my navy blue velvet and we would set off on the thirty minutes walk across the city. In November, it was either raining or had previously rained so that the pavements were always wet. There was no way I could prevent my stockings from getting splashed. I tried walking on my heels and jumping across the puddles, but by the time we arrived the back of my legs would be muddy. It was a disaster without a cure – as if it wasn't bad enough to be a permanent wallflower who was never asked for a dance, unless a boy was told to do so by Mr. Petriss. This exercise was usually performed without a word, except when the boy hissed because I'd stepped on his foot. I was acutely conscious of the state of my legs, of the navy dullness of my frock, and what the boy thought of me. I would miss the rhythm, try to make up for it, and hop like a duck on an icy pond. It was agony. And yet, torn between hope and despair, week after week, I insisted on going to the dance. Aunt Helen must have been ashamed of me, but she made no objection. Learning to dance was a skill I had to acquire whether I was good at it or not, just as I had to learn to play tennis and the piano. As to agonizing over my stockings, I was on my own. She never suggested that I could have another pair to put on when we arrived at the dance.

Yet, if on the Day of Atonement, I had to face a judge, he would not be lenient.

'You abandoned your aunt when she needed you!' he would thunder at me. 'You fled the country and watched her grow old from afar. She developed a cataract on her eye and her heart began to fail. She was in and out of hospitals and wanted to see you. Did you go to Budapest to hold her hand? You had no time. She knew that she was dying. Her past was slowly disintegrating in her memory because nobody was there for whom her life had any meaning. It is terrible to die among strangers. You might find it out for yourself.'

'I know. Don't you think I know? Don't threaten me. Retribution never works so directly.'

'She darned your socks, washed your hair and checked your school reports. She didn't have to do it. You were her sister's child, not her own.'

'I know that. Had she been my mother, she would have bought me a second pair of stockings as a spare.'

10

For the Prince to fall in love with Cinderella after a full beauty treatment by her Fairy Godmother was no big deal. The real thing would have been for him to notice her sitting dejectedly next to her aunt, her stockings splashed with mud and *then* to dance with her all night.

There was an Open Evening and Eva Erdos and her mother brought a guest. He was not a schoolboy like the others but a young man over twenty. I watched him with envy. He was tall and handsome and chatted easily with Eva and her mother. Then, to my surprise he stood up and came towards me. He asked me for a dance and I followed him in a trance. While we carefully negotiated the steps of the foxtrot he told me that his name was Imre Székely and that his mother was a friend of Mrs. Erdos. 'How is it that boys from St Mark college don't mind mixing with you lot?' he asked, 'I thought that this place was strictly for Aryans.'

I eagerly explained that Thursday evenings were an exception. It was a mixed class to which Jewish girls were also admitted.

'So you took up the offer just like that. Don't tell me; I know. Jews tolerate every humiliation in the hope that it's the last one.'

I was taken aback.

'Aren't you Jewish?' I asked.

'Of course I am. That's why I wouldn't be seen dead in this establishment. My mother twisted my arm to escort your friend. Are you sure that Mr Petriss doesn't spray the room to decontaminate it after you've left?'

'But, but… this is the only dancing class we know. I must practice because I'm not very good at dancing,' I stammered.

'I can see that,' he agreed. 'We'd better sit down. You should be dancing the Hora. You don't know what it is, do you? It's the national dance of Israel. Boys and girls in a circle, the more the merrier. You might even enjoy it,' he smiled.

This interchange was different from what I'd imagined a boy would talk about. He told me he was the leader of a group of young Zionists, a movement to which every Jew should belong. Officially, it was a religious youth group, which fooled no-one but which, as yet, the authorities were prepared to tolerate.

'We have contact with Zionist groups in Poland and Germany,' said Imre. 'Hungarian Jews either refuse to believe what is happening there, or they think that Hitler will spare them. The days of the Jews in Europe are numbered. The only chance we have is in Palestine.'

'But how can you go there? Can you get a visa? We can't leave the country!'

'There are ways and means. Why don't you come to a meeting and see what it's all about?'

He returned briefly to Eva and her mother, but then spent the rest of the evening with me. I was elated. Here I was, talking to a young man as if this was the most ordinary thing in the world. I forgot the mud on my stockings and it no longer mattered that I couldn't dance.

He walked Aunt Helen and me home and said that he'd keep in touch. I was dizzy with happiness and sick with anxiety. What if he forgot? What if he never contacted me? We had no telephone. After days of unbearable tension the postman brought a letter addressed to me. It was an invitation to a meeting of a Jewish youth organisation on which he had scribbled a few words. Aunt Helen was not impressed. 'He should have come to the house and paid his respects. We don't know what this so called youth organisation is.' She was about to add that I wasn't allowed to take up the invitation but the look on my face made her change her mind, 'In any case you can't go there on your own, it's not done. I want to see for myself what it's all about.'

I would have gone barefoot across the desert or over the Himalayas to that meeting, but certainly not in her company. I became almost hysterical. In the end, Marinka came to my rescue. She said that she would chaperone me, but she only came as far as the next street corner.

The headquarters of the Zionist youth group was a house in Kiraly Street. I heard the sound of shouting and laughter even before I opened the door. Imre greeted me as an old friend and introduced me to the others. Someone brought more chairs which we arranged in a semi-circle to listen to a man who gave a talk about something, using a lot of statistics. Somebody wound up the gramophone and we all linked hands and danced in a circle. Girls and boys talked easily with each other and behaved as if they'd known me for ages. I was in heaven and prayed that Imre would walk home with me.

I don't remember if he did, but some time later he came on a visit and a desultory conversation with Aunt Helen. It was weeks after this that he kissed me when we were alone in the room. It was true that the kiss missed my mouth and landed on the side of my nose but it meant that now we were a couple, *chaver* and *chavera.* I was faint with happiness. Imre was overwhelmed and didn't know what to say. We were almost relieved when Aunt Helen returned to the room.

There would be many more kisses and cuddling after this, of course – in doorways in the dark, on the back seat of the cinema while I was supposed to be revising Latin with a friend, under the arcades of Parliament, with the Danube gently lapping against the quay. But it never went further than kisses. We didn't know much about contraceptives and the pill hadn't even been thought of. Pregnancy would have been a disaster of such proportion that it is hard to find an equivalent today. All youth movements had strict rules about the relationship between the sexes. We would have to wait until we arrived in Israel.

11

The political situation was going from bad to worse. Many of my friends were joining the illegal Communist party without telling their parents. We covered up for each other but, to Aunt Helen's surprise and grievance, I defied her to attend the meetings after school. She slapped my face, I was rude to her, and we ended up in tears. The day after my school finals I confronted her with the news that I was leaving home to join a Zionist commune. We faced each other like enemies. She looked at me as if I was a stranger and said in a choking voice that she did not want to see me ever again. Neither of us thought of packing a suitcase. I left without anything, apart from a raincoat which, for some reason, I put under my arm. With the remnants of my pocket money I took the streetcar to Buda.

The commune was a *Hachsara,* a preparation for life on a Kibbutz in Israel. The group leader was my friend, Hava Fischer, a pale, bookish girl with a permanent limp as a result of polio, who gave the impression of being much older than her twenty-one years. The commune was housed in a semi-dilapidated villa in the Buda hills, some distance from the cogwheel tram, so that it could be reached only after a good half-hour walk uphill. Property, as everybody knew, was theft. Therefore, all our belongings – coats, clothes and underwear – were communally-owned. Washing was done in the basement laundry by two of the girls, once a week. When it was my turn, my partner and I threw the clothes into a boiling cauldron for ten minutes, took them out and hung them on the line. 'Drip dry' blouses hadn't been invented then and few of the materials were colour-fast, but we knew no-one would complain. Vanity was a bourgeois failing.

In Buda, there was no virgin soil to be broken up so we went to work in town. We had to leave early in the morning because our wages, every penny of which went to the communal fund, were not sufficient for public transport. For a while, I worked in somebody's flat, filling shoulder pads with a spongy material, then in somebody else's bathroom transferring ersatz coffee into nicely labelled jars. The money which I and the other girls earned did not extend to packed sandwiches, and the evening meal was mostly boiled potatoes. Whenever I visited my sister during the day, when Dani was out, I would wolf down anything I found in her kitchen.

'Look at you!' she would cry in despair. 'This blouse is far too big for you and your cardigan is frayed. There's a hole in the elbow!'

'Can I have more noodles?' I would say, trying to twist my socks to hide the hole, which was hopeless since there were more holes than sock.

'And where does this skirt come from?'

'Hava, I think. It's shrunk in the wash. Anyhow, we don't believe in ownership, clothes belong to everybody.' I refused to be concerned about the state of my clothes which, in some obscure way, benefited the state of Israel. In truth I'd been hard-pressed to answer questions about the geography of Palestine, which I vaguely believed to be a thinly populated area, home of nomad tribes and Arabs who would be pleased to have clean drinking water and medical aid. It was life in the kibbutz to which I looked forward. I saw myself with a spade on my shoulder leaving at daybreak in the company of my *chavers* and returning home, tired but happy, to sit around a bonfire under the stars. It would be hard physical work (I'd never tried to do hard physical work before) but I would be part of a commune. Who needed a family? Families were hotbeds of strife and oppression. In the Kibbutz, comradeship was more important than family ties so that even children could choose not to be with their parents.

I'd have rather died on the spot than admit I was exhausted. It was my body which did the protesting. One day, I suddenly fell ill with a high temperature and such violent abdominal pains that the ambulance had to be called. I was taken to hospital where they removed my appendix. When I woke up in a hospital bed there were a lot of people around. A nurse told me that, although my appendix turned out to be perfectly healthy, I'd nearly died under the surgeon's knife because there was an air raid during the operation. With a five inch long scar on my abdomen (thirty years later the surgeon in a Nottingham hospital called the junior doctors to my bedside to see it), I had to leave the commune because I could no longer negotiate the uphill walk.

I would like to forget the next two years. My sister Marinka found some rented accommodation for me and I became a non-paying pupil at Jenny Halasz's one year course for Nursery Nurses. After finishing it, I got a job as a live-in nanny with the wealthy Arnai family.

On Christmas Eve 1943, my employer Eva Arnai and I were decorating the Christmas tree in their elegant room, discussing how much money Eva should give the cook for Christmas. Eva and I had attended the same school, she eight years before me. She was married to a banker who was now in a forced-labour camp but, thanks to heavy bribing, still stationed near Budapest. My charge, five year old Bobo, had been collected by her grandmother that morning, so that she should see the tree in its full splendour for the first time, on Christmas Eve.

'Let's sit down and have some coffee,' Eva said, and I went to the kitchen to make it. When I returned, Eva was unloading a heap of books from a cardboard box. I looked at them longingly.

'I've bought these for you,' she said.

'But so many,' I gasped.

'It's because I'm sacking you. I'm sorry, really sorry. I'd been thinking about it for ages and asked everyone for advice but I see no alternative. I know that Bobo dotes on you and I'd much rather have you around than anyone else, but I'm at the end of my tether. Of course, you can stay until you find another job.' Having finished her speech, she looked relieved, 'Though perhaps not as a nanny,' she added as an afterthought.

I was shaken but not surprised. Bobo had been entertained daily with newly invented games and stories but somehow she seldom had a pair of clean socks which matched. When her mother was not at home, we lived mostly on chocolate and she loved every minute of it. I was in charge of her clothes which Eva said I should have washed by rubbing the dirt out rather than just putting them in the washbasin with her expensive toilet soap. Then there was the problem of never being on time. Once she nearly alerted the police because I was playing cops and robbers with Bobo in the park and forgot to look at my watch. The list was endless. I saw her point.

I moved into digs on the fourth floor of an old house near the Southern Railway station. I was supposed to earn my living from minding a little boy after school and teaching him German.

The lift was permanently out of order, so that my sister Marinka was panting when she opened the door.

'Have you been in bed all day?' she asked pushing away with her foot the clothes in a heap on the floor.

'And all day yesterday,' I admitted miserably. I tried to disappear under the duvet while she opened drawers and looked at my clothes in the wardrobe. She was speechless.

'Could you please telephone Mrs. Engelstein with some excuse?' I asked her as I busied myself with the daily metamorphosis of the bed into a settee. 'I haven't been there since Monday.'

'So you've lost this job too.' Marinka said with resignation, 'Have you had anything to eat?'

I had eaten on the previous day when I had got out of bed to go to the patisserie and spent all my money on a large quantity of cream cakes. Marinka threw the greasy paper into the waste basket which she'd brought me the previous week, together with a hairbrush and some coat hangers. 'I don't know what to do with you.' she sighed.

I didn't know what to do with myself either. Even if I went back to Hajós Street, Aunt Helen wouldn't have had me. Israel suddenly seemed very far away. The sun brought out my freckles every year, so what would I look like in a hot climate?

I had a miserable time. I would stay in bed for days on end without washing, then get up in a panic in the middle of the night to walk the empty streets, a dangerous thing to do. Today my distress would be called a 'nervous breakdown' but at the time it had no name. Like most people in a diffuse state of unhappiness, I found a relatively small but intractable problem to concentrate upon. I thought I was fat and hated myself for it. I begged my sister to find a doctor who would help me lose weight. I trusted the unwritten contract, according to which she would always get me what I wanted, provided I wanted it desperately enough. Marinka resisted for a while but when somebody suggested a specialist in endocrinology we went to see him. The doctor examined me and listened to my woes. He suggested psychoanalysis.

The analyst, Vera Roboz was still working under supervision and accepted me without a fee. I couldn't foresee the bizarre circumstances under which she would save my life. Just then she tried to save my sanity.

I no longer had a home with Aunt Helen but I rediscovered my father's side of the family. After we had left the Márton Street house and moved to St Lőrinc, my father's sister Margit and her daughter Erika moved in.

I rarely saw them, because Aunt Helen and Uncle Nandor and she were not on speaking terms. In the meantime, Aunt Margit's husband had disappeared somewhere in the Ukraine. On my father's suggestion Aunt Margit offered to take me in. I went to live with her and Erika in the Márton Street house in the winter of 1943.

Erika was a year and a half younger than I. When we were children we had played together, but had lost contact as we grew up. Erika was also a Zionist and, because we attended meetings together, we became great friends once more, sharing the same circle of friends.

The news was frightening. Almost every week there were new restrictions and in April, the Jews were ordered to display a yellow star on their chests, the size and material of which was narrowly prescribed. An enterprising acquaintance of Aunt Margit set up a small cottage industry manufacturing yellow stars, and Erika and I were briefly employed by her, cutting the pattern from large sheets of felt. Then, one day, the streets seemed full of yellow blossom as if there were many people sporting a daffodil in their lapels. 'Like branded cattle' Aunt Margit said, but Erika and I found the sight almost funny. 'Once we're in Israel, they'll be displayed in a museum,' Erika said cheerfully, as she sewed the star onto an overcoat.

In fact, there was little hope of ever getting there. Outside Budapest, whole Jewish communities were being rounded up and deported. In Budapest, gangs of Hungarian Nazis, called the 'Arrow Cross,' began to roam the streets checking whether there were any Jews among the pedestrians. Some of their victims, still under the delusion that they were Hungarian citizens, remonstrated with the thugs. 'This is unlawful' – a man, taken at gunpoint, would indignantly shout. 'My identification card is in order! Where are the police?'

My father could have been one of the protesters. 'I'm a Hungarian citizen,' he'd argue 'and, as long as I comply with the regulations, they can't do anything to me.' When he came to Budapest for Sunday lunch, my sister and brother in law begged him not to go home, but he wouldn't listen. On his way there, a fascist gang stopped the streetcar and removed everyone who wore the yellow star. There was no way of making enquiries, but two weeks later, unbelievably, we got a postcard from the transit prison in Sárvár.

'Dear Margit and Vera,' he wrote, 'How are you? I'll try to post you the key from here, because I'll need a few things from home to be sent after me. In the meantime, I could do with a food parcel. Otherwise I'm all right.'

Requiem for Erika - a story.

The old woman who had arrived from England not long previously, tightened the belt of her raincoat and quickened her steps. The narrow road behind Üllői Avenue was badly lit and a steady drizzle blurred the outline of the houses. The street was deserted but even if there had been any passers-by she would not have asked for direction to Márton Street where she was born and where she remained for several months during the war. She could not have forgotten which way to go.

The wet pavement glittered faintly under the street lamps but the rest of the street dissolved in the rain. The houses seemed to turn inwards, guarding the secrets of their staircases and inner corridors. She stretched up to see the plate above the doorway, but all it showed was a number. This was even more distressing than having confused the lions near the bridge with the sphinxes of the Opera House whose anatomy used to puzzle her so much when she was a child.

A gust of wind blew the rain into my face and I would have lost my balance but for a steadying arm around my shoulder. I held on to the knitted glove with the familiar darned patch. My first fleeting thought was for the imitation fur collar which was still the same after more than forty years.

'Watch where you're going!' Erika said, 'The last thing you want is to break your leg. There's nobody around to hear you yelling for help.'

Her face was tense with concern. 'Haven't you got an umbrella?' she asked and pulled me under hers.

'I left it at the airport with the rest of my luggage,' I said. I stopped dead, looking at the house in front of her. I knew it well. The curved iron railings of the main balcony bulged out like a fat man's belly. The balcony was still supported by the torso of a bearded Atlas, now dripping with rain. As a child, I'd been fascinated by his muscular shoulders and non-existent body. But surely this house had been demolished? I clearly remembered the crane hovering above the roof and the scaffolding in front of the boarded up windows. I had wanted to go in but the foreman sternly told me that there was no longer a staircase inside, and that everyone who used to live there was now dead. Yet the house in front of me was as it always had been, only shabbier. Some of the balcony railings had been replaced by straight rods and the plaster giant had lost half his head.

Erika was tugging on my arm. 'Let's go,' she said.

'You should have stayed with me that evening instead of following Leon,' I looked at her accusingly. 'Even if the worst came to the worst, we wouldn't have got separated.'

'Never mind that now,' Erika said, 'Which way are you going?'

'I'm not sure where I am.'

'You're in Tüzoltó Street. Márton Street is further down to the left,' she said as I fell into step with her, 'How come that you've forgotten?'

'I have a theory about it. It's because I've dreamt about it so often. Dreams distort a place. They change narrow streets into avenues and roads into squares so that the landscape gets altered all the time. Stop grinning!'

'Nonsense. You and your theories! You never had a sense of direction. Do you remember the outing to Nagymaros when you bet ten people that the station was on our left?'

'I also remember that trick of yours of unexpectedly turning into a side road while we were walking,' I said crossly. 'I remember when we were on our way to the National Theatre and you turned left while I continued to walk on. You made me miss the first act of 'The Seagull! It was a rotten thing to do.'

'I couldn't help it,' Erika smirked in her collar, 'I was fed up with you for never knowing the way. You should have looked, instead of lecturing me about the difference between agnostics and atheists.'

'When did your hair go grey?' I asked to change the subject, 'Aunt Margit's hair remained black all her life.'

'Mother was always proud of her hair,' Erika remembered with a smile, 'My younger daughter has the same hair, you know. She lives in Berlin and is married to an architect. She had nearly finished her studies when she met him on holiday.'

Her voice became dreamy like the sing-song voice of an adult telling a fairy tale to a child.

'They've got two boys… My younger grandson is especially talented. Have you ever heard Menuhin in performance? He listened to David and decided to take him as his pupil. Isn't it strange how musicality is transmitted in a zigzag line?'

She meant my father, who was the only musical one in the family. Margit, his sister, was practically tone deaf like the rest of them, including Erika.

The drizzle changed into solid rain. I was tightening the hood of my raincoat and missed the beginning of what Erika was saying...

'...because the daughters of my younger son. I'd always wanted a large family, even at eighteen.'

This was not strictly true. When Erika was eighteen and I was nineteen, we didn't think of the children we were going to have. It was 1944, the year when the Budapest Jews were about to be deported. In April, the radio announced that single women who came under the Nuremberg law and had to wear the yellow star, were to be called up. We had to report for paramilitary service within three days, with our personal belongings not exceeding five kilograms. Everyone understood that this meant deportation to camps outside Hungary. Those who feared the worst were talking about hard labour and a harsh regime.

When I arrived home that evening, Erika had already heard the news. She was standing on the tips of her toes on a chair, with her right hand wrapped in a rag trying to fix the pipe of the iron stove. She was tall and slim and wore her ash blonde hair straight in spite of the new fashion for permanent waves. I remember thinking that she looked like a gothic sculpture, one of the wise virgins standing in a semicircle on a cathedral's facade.

'Thank God you're back,' she said as she stepped down and wiped her hand. 'I can't think where mother has gone. She seems to have forgotten about the curfew. Did she tell you that she was going out?'

'I haven't seen her. Stop fretting, she'll back in time. Have you thought about how we'll manage to get everything we need into a backpack? I want to take my heavy boots and some books. How about you?'

'Could she have gone to the Holzhausers? She must have panicked when she heard the news.'

'We have three days left to make arrangements. If those cousins of the Holzhausers really come to live here there would be enough people for Aunt Margit to be allowed to stay in the house. Look! This wretched stove is smoking again. Give me the rag!'

The kitchen door was kicked open and Aunt Margit stumbled in dishevelled and out of breath. Her wiry black hair escaped from her felt hat and the yellow star was dangling half unstuck from her coat. She threw two shopping bags full of potatoes on the floor and collapsed into a chair.

'Dolly Holzhauser is going into hiding,' she said, without a greeting, 'They have an old nanny whose sister lives on a farm. I can't see how anybody can stay unobserved on a farm, can you?'

'Mum, your yellow star is unstuck! You're lucky not to have met a patrol. For God's sake be more careful.'

'Does it matter? Nothing matters any more. Nobody knows where they'll take you. Couldn't we try that solicitor who...'

'It's no use. You know it isn't. Come, have some lentils. There's real meat in it, the butcher's boy put it aside for me.'

Aunt Margit pushed away the plate of lentils. 'I don't want anything. How can you think about food?'

'Don't worry, Auntie, it won't be so bad,' I said wolfing down the lentils, 'They need people to work in the fields now that most of the men have been called up. We'll probably be posted somewhere nearby and come home for the weekends. It might even be nice to work in the open air.'

Aunt Margit shook her head and went into her room. Erika followed her with the plate of lentils. I took the sewing box from the shelf and went to the room I shared with Erika. It was small and narrow but it had an invaluable asset: its window was so low that people could climb in from the street.

I had just bitten off the thread after the last stitch when Erika came in. She had been crying, but sat down on the sofa with a grin. I can't remember exactly what was said but the conversation ran something like this:

'Well, countess, what next?'

'Next to nothing, my lady, next to nothing,' I replied. 'Nothing is the nearest thing to anything goes. Have you taken your Depressol as prescribed?'

'Yes, your Archness, seven tablets with a glass of hemlock, but I remained uncheered.'

'If the symptoms persist you must take an antithesis. It has never failed to help. Take it in a silver spoon.'

'Where there's a silver lining, there must be a spoon.'

'Not fair!' I protested, 'You shouldn't. This wasn't a proverb.'

'Yes it was.'

'Hush, be quiet!' she said. There was a knock at the window. We both jumped. This was what we were listening for all the time.

'It'll be Eli,' I said, switching off the light, 'He said he'd probably be able to come after curfew.'

Erika was already undoing the blackout blind. She turned back and whispered, 'It's Leon.'

Strangely, I wasn't disappointed. I must have been a little in love with Leon myself. I took a deep breath when Erika opened the window. The fresh night air came into the room bringing messages of spring from the chestnut trees of Üllői Avenue and the park behind.

Leon jumped down to the floor. 'The Arrow Cross was patrolling the street,' he said, 'I haven't seen so many of them before in this area. They must be multiplying like locusts.' He kissed Erika on the cheek. 'It's your good luck, darling, that they didn't see me.'

'Would you like some coffee?' I asked, edging towards the door, 'We've got a bit of white sugar left.'

'I'd like some, but not just now. Please don't go, we have to talk.'

He turned to Erika.

'Is your mother asleep?'

Erika nodded. 'I hope so. She's taken a lot of sleeping pills. She can't sleep without them any longer.' Suddenly she brightened up. 'Do you know that Mrs Roth next door is spreading rumours about men climbing through our window at night? You're ruining our reputation.'

'A poor girl's only asset,' Leon grinned as he sat down.

'And how shall I make a good match without it?' giggled Erika. Her face was flushed and her eyes sparkled. Her eyebrows were as finely pencilled as the downy fur on Dürer's drawing of a hare. She was sitting next to Leon on the sofa with barely an inch between them. Leon made a movement as if he wanted to embrace her, then jumped up and went to the window.

'Your blackout arrangements are lousy,' he said examining the canvas, 'but it doesn't matter. You can't stay here. I hope you weren't seriously thinking of reporting for slave labour? I've managed to get you some papers. Birth certificates, identity cards, police registration, the lot.'

I should have known, I thought, that if anyone could save us, it would be him. All the men I knew had been made helpless by the monstrous régime. All but Leon.

'I'm afraid you and Erika have to separate,' he said to me as he handed over the documents. 'You're going to be Magda Kovács, apprentice hairdresser from Kolozsvar, looking for a job in Budapest. Father: János Kovács, mother: Julia Kis. You must learn all the details by heart.'

'And Erika?'

'She'll come with me. Pity I can't take you both. Now listen. You'll leave the house Thursday morning at eight and go to the Catholic church in Üllői Avenue. A woman will be waiting for you and take you to a safe house. Her name is Maria. Don't worry, you'll recognise her,' he said, when I was about to interrupt. 'She's a big girl, peroxide blonde, in her late thirties. You mustn't wear the yellow star of course.'

'But how am I going to leave the house without it?'

'Think of something! Use your brain! Will you expect to be told what to do next all the time?' he said crossly, then relented:

'Take a pair of scissors with you and remove the star inside the church.'

Erika had been listening to all this in a daze but now she found her voice.

'Hold on! The two of us are going together or we won't go. We won't be separated.'

It was a relief. I wanted to hug her.

'Wouldn't it be safer to report for labour, even it is going to be hard labour somewhere?' I asked.

Leon was walking up and down the room, five steps each way.

'What incredible fools you are! Where do you think they are going to take you?'

'They need people on the farms...there's a shortage of manpower.'

'Which they are going to solve with the help of wailing Jewesses who couldn't lift a shovel?' Leon said with scorn, 'You'll be put on a train and taken to Germany where you'll be killed. I've lived through it in Poland while you were all sitting here in a fool's paradise. Don't you understand that you've no choice?' he shouted in sudden fury.

His anger filled the room. I was shattered and so, it seemed, was Erika. There had been rumours about mass murders in Poland but nobody knew what to believe. We suddenly understood that what Leon said was true.

'But my mother....What will happen to her if I defy the summons?'

'The same that'll happen if you report for deportation,' Leon said curtly. 'Still, her chances are better if you live than if you die.'

He gave his handkerchief to Erika to dry her eyes.

'You'll be safe with me,' he promised.

The rain became heavier with every minute. A sudden wind attacked us like a spectre darting out from several corners at once. Erika held on to me.

'He never made love to me you know,' she said, 'Not properly, I mean. He had seen in Poland what happened to pregnant women. In any case, one's chances of survival were much better if one was not. Do you remember? There was no such thing as a safe method.'

She had no umbrella and the raindrops running down her face looked like tears. I had to swallow before I asked: 'Somebody else then? You were almost ashamed to be still a virgin.'

'Oh, it's of no importance. Every dog has its day, as they say, and I had mine. Vienna...I went there to study painting after the war...It was spring and the fruit trees in Grinzing were all in bloom. I had a blue crépe de chine frock and a white belt... Hans Friedrich couldn't take his eyes off me. I have seen the bank of the Danube in moonlight and heard the song of the cicadas rising and ebbing like sighs.'

...Studied painting? Erika couldn't paint. Once she sent me a postcard from a holiday camp with a pencil sketch of the tent. I've still got it in a box among old letters and photographs which survived the upheavals of my life.

'You wanted to travel and see the world,' I said, 'You wanted to see the sea and the Alps and wanted to go to Paris. Do you remember our game of sticking a pin, blindfold, into a map?'

'But I did travel. I travelled a great deal. I was invited all over the world to talk about the Institute. I was right to have a career instead of a family. I couldn't have been so successful if I'd had children of my own.'

'Your daughter in Berlin. Her son is a pianist?'

Perplexed, Erika lifted her hand to her fine ash blond hair. She twirled it between her finger and thumb with the slow movement I knew so well. She was eighteen, warm and gay, like a young deer ready to run.

'I can have as many futures as there are colours in a prism,' she tossed her head, 'I haven't told you about my travels to Canada or my business career, or about the farm. Did you know what riding a horse feels like? It's like being carried through air… stop crying! Must old women always blubber like a tap dripping?'

'One has to come to terms with death,' I said, 'whether one has lived out one's life or not. The tears of the survivors after Thermopylae, the Crusades, the Battle of the Somme, have dried up long ago. I'm crying because by now I'm the only one who knows that you ever lived.'

But as I was talking I realised that she'd turned into Márton Street and was gone.

In Memoriam Erika Mann 1925-1944

12

Leon's friend Maria was waiting for me in the Catholic church and took me to a safe house in Zugló, a prosperous middle class district on the other side of Budapest. The safe house was a furnished apartment on the second floor in a quiet tree-lined street, with a tree directly below the window. Two young Poles and Maria, who was the girlfriend of one of them, were the residents. Others came and went, seldom bothering to tell me the name they'd chosen. It could become handy for escape since the men had belts which would hook into a window bar. (These belts also had a steel file hidden in them which could cut through an iron grille, but I only learned about that later).

In the front room there was a printer, and several duplicating machines, on which identity cards and resident permits were produced. The two young men from Poland knew a little Hungarian but they needed somebody who was fluent in the language and wouldn't make spelling mistakes. I was also to be a courier, taking the papers to various addresses after dark to avoid a chance encounter with somebody who might notice that I wasn't wearing the yellow star.

They didn't tell me much about the organization, which provided an escape route to Romania, from where people hoped to reach Israel. They needed new identification cards and travelling permits, which involved bribing a lot of people, including policemen, customs officers and border guards. Now I understood Leon's grandiose gesture when he'd thrown a handful of jewels on the table to impress Erika. Wealthy Jewish families had to pay heavily, because they also had to pay for those who had no money. We didn't cook – I don't even remember if there was a kitchen – but lived on groceries bought by Maria who was a genuine Aryan and could be sent out to do the shopping.

I'd known fear before – fear of exams, fear of being found out when skiving – but this was different. It did not feel like fear, it felt like an alien body in my stomach which made me gasp for air and prevented me from eating. I rapidly began to lose weight and developed a self-assurance which

I'd never had before. There was a lot of laughter and bravado in the safe house, also acts of bravery, like that of Leon and two others who'd put on a German uniform and, pretending to be Nazi officers, brought back their comrades from a prison camp. Leon visited the safe house occasionally but Erika was somewhere at the border escorting people across.

I had no idea what the rest of my family was doing. It was like living on the top of a mountain where the air was thinner and life's ordinary concerns did not reach me. I felt a little drunk all the time, flirting with everyone, and had some trouble keeping my comrades out of my bed. Fear turned into euphoria, euphoria turned into fear. I learned that they are often the same.

It occurred to me that a good way to change my appearance would be to have my hair dyed. I had never before had such a good excuse for doing it! On a hot afternoon I walked boldly into a hairdresser's salon and asked to have my hair dyed blonde. (I later remembered that the owner cast a dubious glance on my chest where the yellow star should have been. Red hair was more prevalent among Jews). An assistant put peroxide on my hair, covered it with a cap and told me to wait until the original colour had bleached out. I waited patiently for a long time but didn't dare to call him. Eventually, he returned and calmly told me that it was closing time. He said he would finish the job the next day and removed the cap from my hair which hung limp and colourless, like wet straw. I didn't want to risk a confrontation and meekly allowed him to tie an old scarf around my head before I left the shop.

Outside it was pouring with rain and I stumbled into a puddle which splashed my legs and skirt with mud. That'll teach me to tell my comrades how glamorous I'll be on my return, I thought crossly, as I waited for the tram to take me back. The tram was crowded and I was squeezed into the back of the platform where I stood dejectedly, when in front of me a man called out in alarm:

'Stop the tram! The head of that woman is on fire!'

This was interesting. I craned my neck to see it, undeterred by the smarting sensation on top of my scalp where the peroxide had begun to smoulder. Before I knew what was happening, I found myself pushed off the tram and under a leaking gutter from which a steady stream of water was pouring over my head. I don't know why this incident remains with me, but I remember it whenever I take a callous interest in somebody else's calamity and realize that the 'burning head' could just as easily be mine.

The Gestapo came one evening when only the two Poles, Maria and I were in the flat. There was a knock at the door and Maria went to investigate through the spy window. She only saw the concierge, who was bribed and could be let in, so she opened the door. The concierge stepped aside allowing three plain clothes men to push past Maria. They had guns and ordered us to face the wall, spread-eagled, while they searched the flat. With dozens of fake identity cards on the table and printers and duplicators all around the room there was not much searching to do and, seeing that there was no resistance, they relaxed. The next thing I remember was that one of them told me quite kindly to pack an overnight case and take my handbag with me. The only one to protest was Maria; the Poles knew better.

In front of the house, two taxi cabs were waiting for us. I was told to sit in the first one, next to the driver, while two of the detectives settled themselves in the back. The drivers (genuine taxi drivers, angry but obedient) were told to drive to the Gestapo headquarters in Buda. There was no need for a detailed address. The two luxury apartment houses on the hill, taken over by the Gestapo, were notorious.

By that time it was quite late, a beautiful, warm summer evening with people strolling at leisure along the street. When the taxi reached the Danube a man pointed at us. Was he envious of the idle rich who could afford to travel in a taxi? The two detectives behind me were talking to each other and did not bother about me. I slowly opened the handbag in my lap to extract an unfinished identity card with the stamped photograph of my boyfriend Eli Bohrer. I knew that when we arrived I would be asked questions and I had no intention of refusing to answer. The Gestapo could have all the information I had, which was practically nothing, but I wanted to keep Eli out of it. Pretending to use my handkerchief I stuffed the photograph into my mouth and began to chew. The cardboard blank wasn't too bad but the taste of the photograph was vile. Still, I managed to eat every bit of Eli's identity card before we arrived.

The Gestapo headquarters were floodlit with uniformed guards swarming at the entrance. Maria, who'd travelled in the taxi behind me, was separated from the Poles and taken to another part of the building while I was escorted to one of the luxury apartments on the third floor.

Although there was no furniture in it, the two bedroomed apartment counted as a luxury one in the 1940s. The view from the windows was spectacular. The parquet floor had an inlaid pattern and there was a kitchenette with an electric cooker and a bathroom tiled to the ceiling, both with running hot water. The Gestapo used it as a temporary prison for the wives and children of recently arrested VIPs. It was there that wives of dissenting politicians and rich industrialists waited to learn about the fate of their husbands who were questioned in another part of the building. When the interrogation also concerned hidden money and valuables, the wife would also be sent for questioning. Two of them were so badly beaten that they were carried back in a blanket.

It was late at night when I arrived. The others had bedded themselves and their children on the bare floor, as best as they could, and many were asleep. Somebody switched on the light and a slim young woman made room for me on the floor. To her amazement, I still had the overnight bag on me and offered her some of its contents as a pillow, which she gratefully accepted.

Trying to get to sleep on the hard floor proved difficult, especially since a child wailed continuously. It was little girl of seven with earache, She was in great pain. Her mother was in despair. 'My darling, my darling, I wish I could take the pain from you,' she kept repeating, 'Mummy I wouldn't mind if you did for a bit,' the child sobbed. The duty policeman who sat, wooden-faced, inside the entrance did not respond to entreaties to find a doctor or at least some aspirin. 'I haven't been ordered to do it,' he said.

In the morning, everyone took turns in the bathroom, but those who had children with them found it hardest to wait. In any case, children made the overcrowding even more intolerable. Everyone's nerves were frayed by the bored and frightened children, about eight of them, crying, clinging, and sulking. It was not for nothing, however, that I had received nursery-school training the year before. I suggested that the adults move into one room and made the other into a makeshift nursery where even the older children were delighted to play games and listen to stories. I distributed the contents of my suitcase because it was very hot and most people had been given no time, when arrested, to pack a change of underwear. The wife of a diplomat at the French embassy who had made room for me on the floor the first night kissed and hugged me for it. 'I'll give you slips of pure silk with Brussels lace when the war is over,' she promised. I never saw her again.

The children were sitting cross-legged on the floor while I narrated the adventures of János the Hero from the epic poem that we all knew. The dreaded door opened and a policeman asked for me by name. I choked in the middle of a word and began to tremble as I followed the messenger. Several days had gone by since my arrest. I had learned through the grapevine that the two Poles had filed through the iron bars of a window in the basement where the male prisoners were kept. They escaped, taking others with them. I wondered what kind of pressure I would be under to reveal their plans.

The detective dealing with my case was Hungarian. He was sitting behind a desk and looked ordinary, like a clerk or a salesman. He asked me why I was trembling.

'I'm frightened,' I said, 'I don't want to be taken to a death camp in Germany. I'm too young to die.'

This made him angry. 'Who is talking about dying? You Jews are frightening yourselves with stupid rumours. It will do you good to be sent to a labour camp to do some work which you've probably never done in your life. Show me your hands!'

He was rummaging in the handbag which had been taken from me when I arrived.

'Aha! So you're a junkie!' he cried, satisfied. He took out morphine ampoules and a syringe from a box.

'Junkie?' I asked, in genuine surprise, 'Why would I be a junkie?'

'Are you telling me that this doesn't belong to you?'

'Of course it belongs to me. My boyfriend stole it for me from an infirmary because when it comes to the worst I want to commit suicide. But I've never found out what to do with the syringe.'

This was so stupid that it stunned him. He asked me about the safe house but he knew more about it than I did. He unzipped the side of the handbag and found a photograph of my pretty mother, taken when she was nineteen.

'My mother,' I said, 'She died when I was little.'

By this time, I had calmed down. This was like an ordinary conversation and I sensed in him some goodwill towards me. He scrutinised my mother's photograph while I told him that I'd left school two years previously and what I had done since then.

'This lady doesn't look Jewish,' he said helpfully, 'It's definitely an Aryan face.'

'Oh no, you're mistaken,' I said, secure in the knowledge that I was right, 'Everyone in my family is Jewish.'

When I recalled the conversation later I could have hit my head against the wall but I also think that from then on he believed me. If my comrades had planned their escape from the Gestapo, I'd certainly be the last person to be told.

A few days later he sent for me again. I sat down with a feeling that it was going to be a normal conversation and I was right. He asked me how I'd got involved with the people in the flat and I told him. I relaxed so much that I asked him why he'd joined the Gestapo.

'As a matter of fact I didn't,' he said, 'I'm a policeman and had no say in it when I was transferred.' He explained that he disagreed with the excesses of the Germans, but something had to be done because the Jews wanted to take over the country. Jews never did a day's work in their lives, they became rich by making others work for them. With no risk of being contradicted by his audience, he harangued me about a Jewish conspiracy, and genuinely seemed to believe that the purpose of the concentration camps was to teach the Jews how to work.

Suddenly, the door opened, and two German officers came in without knocking. My detective jumped up to stand attention than shouted at me:

'Clean the sink over there! Are you deaf? Move!'

I went to the sink but not quite understanding that this was for the benefit of his visitors, I said that it didn't need cleaning. He followed me and slapped my face very hard, then opened the door and gave me a push, shouting to a guard to take me back. I didn't see him again. I should, I suppose, remember him with gratitude.

Eventually I was transferred to an inner city prison the name of which I don't remember. It was painful to part from my new friends but we promised – somewhat dubiously – to meet again after the war.

I was escorted downstairs where a prison van was waiting. The back door was high but I scrambled in somehow and looked around. All the seats were occupied. Some people seemed in a state of shock, while others were conversing in a low voice. The guard in the back looked bored and took no notice of them. A young man shifted to make room for me on the bench. He was unshaven with closely cropped hair, and he grinned at me, showing his gold teeth.

'I know you,' he said, 'Your father has a shop in St Lőrinc. My mother used to buy corn for the chicken there.' His face had an unhealthy pallor but he wore an expensive looking suit and a gaudy necktie. There was no yellow star on his chest. When I sat down he offered me an apple from a paper bag beneath his seat.

'Thank you,' I said gratefully. 'I don't know when I'll have an apple again. I don't think they're on the prison menu!'

'This one isn't too bad,' he said, as he took another apple from the bag. 'The food comes from an outside canteen because it's only a transit place.'

'How do you know?' I asked, surprised, 'Have you been there before?'

'Haven't I just?' he grinned, 'It's by no means the worst place. You're allowed parcels and visitors from the start.'

'But you're not Jewish, are you?'

'Not bloody likely,' he answered with dignity, pulling himself up on his seat, 'I'm a criminal.'

'A criminal?' I asked stupidly, 'What do you mean?'

'A professional criminal. Don't look so surprised. I'm a burglar. It's a job like any other, only sometimes you get caught. I haven't been very lucky recently and the bastards gave me two years. What about you? Have you been sentenced?'

I shook my head, 'Jews don't get a trial.'

'Shocking, isn't it? I don't hold with it at all. I've been just saying the other day to a pal that Jews are people like us, I really did.'

'By the way, how's your old man?'

I had no wish to talk about it. 'Fine, thank you,' I said.'

'You've changed a lot,' said the burglar scanning me appreciatively, 'I'll tell you something. It's advice. If you have money on you don't try to hide it because the first thing they'll do will be a body search. Better hand it in straight away. They'll let you keep some of it and you'll get privileges. Some warders will even buy things for you.'

This was a blow. When they'd arrested me, I had my mother's jewellery sewn into the lining of my anorak. Jews were supposed to have surrendered their valuables long ago. To my relief, I hadn't been searched at the Gestapo headquarters so that the jewels were still on me. Now they could become my undoing.

'Body search? You mean they strip you?'

'Especially pretty girls like you. I wish I could be there,' he grinned. He tried to put his arm around my shoulder but I recoiled, desperately trying to work out what to do with the jewels. The prison van seemed to take ages to reach its destination and the burglar kept talking. I don't remember much of the conversation, but the outcome was an offer to marry me.

I thought I'd misheard him. 'What do you mean, marry?'

'That's what I said. I could ask the prison chaplain to splice us so that you'd become the wife of an Aryan. What do you say?'

It was a genuine offer, and the way he saw it, a generous one. I don't know how I'd have responded if I thought that marrying him would have saved my life, but I knew that being married to an Aryan did not save anybody. Thinking back, I can only hope that I was not too rude to the young man who was ready to enter into such a misalliance to save me.

Advice from an expert can be invaluable. The first thing I did in the prison was to ask for the toilet where I removed the jewels from the lining of my coat and wrapped them in some crumpled old newspapers which I picked up off the floor.

The room where they searched the new arrival was crowded. I threw the crumpled newspaper into a corner and joined the queue of women waiting to undress. A warder picked up the clothes and expertly turned them inside out. I was told to put them on again since we were not given prison clothes – exactly as my suitor-burglar had told me. No-one took any notice when, on the way out, I picked up the crumpled newspaper off the floor.

It was all in vain, of course. In Auschwitz, it was of no help to have my mother's jewels on me.

Amala and Kamala - a story.

They were nightclub hostesses whom I met in prison during the last year of the war. We spent less than a day together in a communal cell, yet I remember them well because they were the most beautiful girls I had ever seen. One was fair-haired with a porcelain complexion; the other had curly brown hair and the dreamy eyes of an Eastern princess. Both looked elegant and sophisticated, well aware that their contrasting looks made them the perfect foil for the other's beauty.

I can recall their appearance, from their exquisitely lacquered fingernails to the tips of their lizard skin shoes, but I can't remember what they were called. 'Amala' and 'Kamala' force themselves on my memory, blotting out their real names.

First, let me tell you about the real Amala and Kamala.

In 1922 people in the village of Godamur in India told a preacher about the strange creatures they'd spotted near a wolf's den in the forest. The preacher, Rev. Singh, went with them to investigate.

Concealed by the twilight, the small party crept near the den from which two fully grown wolves emerged. They were followed by two cubs and two unidentifiable creatures on all fours, their faces half hidden by long manes.

These were human children, living with the wolves. When cornered, they made menacing noises, shaking their heads left and right like frightened animals. Spitting and snarling, they fought against being captured. Amala died shortly after their capture but Kamala lived for seven more years. The Rev. Singh recorded her development in his diary.

Initially neither child could tolerate daylight and would not sleep for longer than about four hours a day. Although their spines were not deformed they could not walk, but spent most of their time squatting and picking up beetles off the ground. They had two methods of moving forward: elbow and kneecap for small distances, hands and feet for running. At first, they took their nourishment in a crouching position, lapping up fluids with their tongues. It took Kamala six months to reach out with her hands for food, about a year to stand upright while holding on to something. Over the years she learnt to understand most of what she was told and by the end of her short life she had a vocabulary of about fifty words. Nobody knew why these unfortunate children had been abandoned in the forest. The Rev. Singh was convinced that, but for the terrible circumstances which rendered her practically an idiot, Kamala would have been a normal child.

As you see, they had nothing in common with the hostesses of the Moulin Rouge in Budapest who were tall long-legged beauties with the kind of figure which makes men turn round and stare. When the prison warder opened the grille of the communal cell they walked in nodding their thanks as if she'd carried out some menial service. We surrounded them for news but they couldn't tell us anything new. The German army hadn't collapsed and the deportation of the Jews was going on as before.

Their arrest was a commonplace one: they had run into someone in the street who had known Amala from old, who denounced them to the nearest patrol.

'We'd decided from the start that we wouldn't wear the yellow star,' Kamala explained, 'Amala (she used, of course, her friend's real name) looks like a textbook illustration of the perfect Aryan. As for me, I look so Jewish that no-one who saw me without the yellow star could believe that I dared do so.'

She grinned and turned to Amala.

'Do you remember the colonel who kept asking you whether I had Arab blood and promised to keep the secret?'

They giggled, although the joke was on them. We were in a transit prison for petty criminals, prostitutes and Jewish women rounded up for deportation. From time to time a prison van would arrive without warning to take people away.

'You can send a message from here,' I advised them. 'The warder who brought you in can be bribed to post a letter.'

'We've already done that,' Amala said. 'It cost me a ring. She promised to make a phone call as well.'

Their arrest had shaken them but they wanted none of my commiseration. Kamala was sure that their friends would soon get them out. I believed her. They must have had influential friends who could pull strings for them. I've never seen underwear like theirs, silk with hand-made lace.

A few years earlier I would have admired and envied them even more. They were part of the fabulous world of the Moulin Rouge, the nightclub where the then Prince of Wales spent his evenings in the company of Mrs. Simpson. One could read little for weeks on end, other than the story of the Prince who had given up his crown for love. I only had to shut my eyes to see the romantic couple dancing the tango in each other's arms while the Prince's entourage cast dark glances towards Mrs. Simpson. Were they plotting her demise? They must have had spies behind the folds of the velvet curtain.

There was a lot of coming and going in the prison. Prisoners were called out and new ones brought in, bewildered and desperate. Someone returning from the corridor reported that two prison vans had arrived in the courtyard and that a man with a list in his hand had gone to see the warder.

Amala and Kamala, whose expensive scent distinguished them from the rest of us like an invisible screen, did not jump up nervously to hear the news and rumors brought by newcomers every time the door opened. It was I who approached them. Unlike most people around me, I didn't dismiss the rumours of mass executions in the concentration camps. My cousin Erika's boyfriend was a Pole who had witnessed the 'final solution' before he escaped and I knew what happened to the deported.

'Aren't you scared?' I asked Kamala, who was sitting on a bunk bed next to her friend, 'What if they take you away before your friends find out where you are?'

She yawned. 'Wherever we go there will be men. Men are the same everywhere.'

She grinned at Amala. 'I'm not easily frightened. Are you?'

Amala leaned back against the wall to contemplate her perfect feet. 'I don't think so. As long as there are men wherever we are taken, we'll be all right.'

'You're lucky to be together,' I said enviously, thinking of my cousin Erika. 'Have you been friends for long?'

'Ever since I can remember,' said Amala, 'We're both from Kiskoros. Kamala's people are orthodox Jews. Her mother has six children, has her hair shaved, and wears a wig. Isn't it a scream?'

Kamala's face darkened. 'You've no right to talk about her like that. They're religious but at least my father didn't run away when he went bankrupt.' A red patch began to spread around her neck.

'But you despise them! 'Amala said, aghast, 'What about the champagne party when your father publicly disowned you?'

Kamala had tears in her eyes. 'They've gone, you idiot,' she cried. She turned to me to explain. 'They were all deported when the ghetto in Kiskoros was evacuated. Have you got a hankie?' she asked.

'Here, it's clean. You've no experience. Otherwise you'd have hidden one in your sleeve. Come, stop crying. Better tell me about the Moulin Rouge. What was it like?'

But I didn't hear the answer because the warder came in accompanied by a man who read out names from a list and mine was one of them.

I was taken to Sárvár, a small township near the border where thousands of people were waiting for deportation. Some died in the locked carriage of the cattle wagon before we arrived at Auschwitz and saw the legend on the gate:

ARBEIT MACHT FREI

I saw Amala – or was it Kamala? once more for a brief moment a few weeks later. It was in a sandy enclosure as I waited with hundreds of others for transfer to another camp. Amala sat hunched on the ground hunting for lice in her prison clothes. It could have been Kamala since their shaven heads and dirty, emaciated faces made people almost indistinguishable. Kamala looked vacantly in my direction, but did not recognise me.

Part Two

TO BE TWENTY

1

The disused brick factory at Sárvár was a transit prison for hundreds of people awaiting deportation. People on bunk beds, people in the corridors, people in the yard, bundles, suitcases and backpacks everywhere. It was pandemonium, with babies crying, people arguing and the military police shouting orders. Nobody knew what would happen; only that it would be bad. I have no recollection of how many days I spent there, only that on the day when the cattle trucks came I flattened myself into a six inch deep recess in the brick wall in an attempt to hide. The military policeman who pulled me out shook his head at such foolishness.

The platform at Sárvár station was cordoned off to keep the local people out. They gathered to watch the long line of cattle trucks with one guard pulling, another pushing people into the gaping mouth of the coach. Curiously, all this went on in silence. Even babies and young children became rigid with fear so that the only sound was the shouting of the guards. The silence of hundreds of people waiting to be deported must have been an eerie experience for the small crowd watching us. 'But why are they so silent?' asked a woman leaning across the gate which separated us. 'Can't you see?' somebody answered, 'Because they know that they're guilty, that's why.'

Inside the truck there was standing room only, but soon after the door was closed with a bang and a kick to make it secure, people began to collapse so that finally everybody was crouching on the floor. The August sun blazed on the tin roof of the truck which was almost dark inside because the iron bars of the opening near the roof had been camouflaged with twigs. I was nearly in the lap of a young man with skullcap and orthodox ear-locks who was horrified by being so close to a woman. He muttered angry curses when I took off my blouse but, just before I lost consciousness, he laboriously took out a flask from his pocket and gave me a sip of some strong spirit. It took the train three days to reach its destination but I must have been unconscious for most of the time since I don't remember much of it.

For a while a baby screamed; then it stopped. Much later, perhaps on the second day, the train slowed down and came to a halt at a disused station. A boy passing by pulled aside the twigs on the window out of curiosity. I can still see the look of horror on his gaunt adolescent face when people inside the truck began to scream for water. He ran to get a bucket of water and a tin mug which he managed to push through the rails. As soon as the mug was within the grasp of the outstretched arms everyone tried to grab it, spilling the water, every drop of it. I think the boy tried again, but the guards came and chased him away.

How do I know that it was an abandoned railway station? Probably because, once or twice during the journey, we were let out to relieve ourselves on the grass. That, like the communal latrine in the disused brick factory in Sárvár, was of no use to me. The taboo connected with bodily functions was so strong that a few months previously, when my boyfriend and I had managed to be alone in the Buda hills at last, neither of us dared to disappear for a pee. By an unspoken agreement, we returned earlier than planned. The military policemen who guarded us didn't even look away when men and women, old and young, stumbled out of the train to squat down in the grass.

By the end of the journey, I had only two thoughts left. One was of stewed pears. Stewed pears in a large glass jar in the pantry. Pears sliding around on a plate in their own juice. Stewed pears could be bought in tins, and my mother's jewellery was still secure in the lining of my anorak. Wherever we were going, somebody could be bribed to get stewed pears for me.

My other thought was of air. How was it that I had never before appreciated how sweet it was to breathe? Never mind where they are taking us, eventually they would have to open the door and there would be air. Air above me, air around me, square miles of air, and whatever happened afterwards I would still be able to breathe.

Many people have written about the arrival to Auschwitz. Expert hands unbolted the doors and began to sort out the amorphous mass of humanity vomited out by the coaches. They separated men from women, children from adults, old from young, with speed and efficiency. The monstrous harvesting machine of Auschwitz gobbled up people like identical ears of corn. I cannot add much to it because my memory deceives me. I remember a noisy glass-covered hall of enormous proportions like a railway station, extending a hundredfold, in which rivers of people streamed to and fro shouting in many languages. German soldiers and convicts in striped prison uniforms who, I thought, couldn't be prisoners because they gave us orders, came between the multitude sorting and separating them. An endless column of women and children moved slowly ahead, children crying, men shouting and arguing. There were fires burning in the distance, emitting much smoke.

It was not so. I know now that there was no roof above us, that there were no fires and what I remember as smoke was probably morning or evening dusk. My memory also holds the image of two young children – a boy of seven and a girl of five – whose mother was stepping back from the slowly moving column to slide into the queue of unattached women, yet I know that I never saw them. It was much later, their mother told me, told everybody, wanting the world to hear, that, in order to save her own life, she had abandoned her children to the gas chamber.

We slept in a huge barn-like building in which hundreds of women had to find a place for the night on the concrete floor. The simplest way to torture a large number of people is to put them into a space with insufficient room for them all, and then to leave them to fight with fists and elbows, sobbing and shouting in the dark until weakness and exhaustion overtake them.

The shower had pipes on the ceiling, but no taps. We were given a small piece of grey soap; the water was then switched on and switched off again. We were told to strip naked and leave all our belongings (including my anorak with my mother's jewellery tucked once more into the lining) except for our shoes, which we had to put on again. The prisoners in charge of the newcomers urged us to hurry up while they sorted the clothes into mountains of blouses and skirts, hills of bras and panties. In the next room (or was it in another building?) we were shaved. I marvelled at the hair on the floor, which was like a hairdresser's except that the hair was knee deep. Blonde and brunette curls and pigtails mingled prettily with each other in a soft heap, which almost invited you to bounce on it. My armpit and pubic hair disappeared under the diligent hands of women sitting saddle-fashion on chairs and working as if on a production line. We left the building one by one to form a queue again. But this was a different queue because suddenly everyone looked the same. Was it at that stage that striped prison clothes were distributed to us? According to my memory we were naked when we lined up for selection, but those who could verify this are no longer here.

I was standing there bald and naked, yet humiliation was the last thing bothering me. I wanted to live. There was some reassurance in the long, undulating line of shaven heads and naked bodies. I was part of the multitude and so many people, I believed, would be impossible to kill.

There was neither a tree nor a blade of grass to be seen between the rows and rows of identical buildings, as if nature itself had ceased to exist. The August sun glared cruelly as the queue moved on. We were told (there were interpreters, but rumours rippled over the group even before the announcement) that we were going to be inspected for fitness to work. The work would be heavy, only suitable for young and healthy women.

I looked around. What would happen to those who were unfit for work?

They would be given easy tasks, working in the kitchen or on cleaning duties.

The queue filed past a man in a doctor's white coat. Each time he pointed at a woman, it came to a halt. She then had to step out of the queue and join a separate group. Dr Mengele often turned to explain his work to the two German girls in nurses' uniform, on either side of him. A quick glance was enough for him to guess a prisoner's age or to notice a limp or a slight deformity. He looked at me from the corner of his eye and commented, 'Schwanger'.

My German was good enough to understand that the word meant 'pregnant'. It was an understandable mistake because my belly had swollen up during the journey in the cattle truck. But I couldn't be pregnant! The momentous question – whether I should 'go all the way' with my boyfriend – was what I'd been agonising about for ages on the analyst's couch. Psychoanalysts were not supposed to give direct advice but Vera Roboz firmly forbade it. She didn't argue or explain but threatened to end the treatment if I had sex. I'd stormed at her and called her names without understanding her reasons, which only became clear here in Auschwitz. Halfway to the group of those deemed unfit I turned back to face Mengele.

'Ich bin doch eine Jungfrau!' I cried. Virgins couldn't be pregnant.

He must have been fed up with the interminable queue behind me because he just shrugged and let me return to the line.

What if my German had not been good enough to understand the word 'schwanger'? But I had loved the German language since my early childhood. Like many others in the newly emerging middle classes of the Austro-Hungarian Monarchy, my grandparents had gradually changed from their native Yiddish into educated German. My father denied that he understood any Yiddish. Yiddish was the language of poverty and pogroms, rituals and frequent pregnancies, while German was the language of culture and affluence, radiating from Vienna across the Monarchy.

My parents had a little German and spoke a few sentences over my head if they didn't want me to understand. I became all ears, eager to get the key to the language in which adult mysteries were told. German nursery rhymes in the private play school sounded like spells and ritual incantations, and added to the magic. I loved German poems which transported me to the Rhine, shimmering in the sunset, and to the dark forest where the father was forever galloping towards his doom. As a child I had only to shut my eyes to see the mountain pass where the horse Falada commiserated with the lost princess:

> ***If your mother knew what they've done to you***
> ***Her heart would surely break...'***

I understood what Dr. Mengele had said – but my relief at the time was not as great as when I recall it now. Easier jobs were tempting, and working in a kitchen might not have been so bad. I only half-believed that the women who had been separated from the rest of us, were going to the gas chamber. There is a twilight zone between knowing and not knowing, as German civilians could also have told you at the time.

Death was for the old. In Auschwitz, it was also for the weak and the disabled, but I was neither. I felt much more threatened by the hostility of my own body which, like a hibernating animal, ceased both to take in food and eliminate it. I was able to drink the dark liquid called coffee and could urinate, but for more than three weeks I hadn't excreted anything. I offered the black bread they gave us to my new friend Anna.

'I won't take it. Force yourself to eat it,' she insisted, swallowing hard. Anyone else would have snatched the bread out of my hand, but Anna was a communist with high moral standards. She too had been questioned by the Gestapo, but hadn't been let off as lightly as I. Torture had made her determined to keep her humanity at all costs. She refused to fight for a space or to fawn on the working prisoners whose job it was to distribute the food. Day after day, she tried to persuade me to eat my ration. Later we got separated and by the time I'd heard that she'd died, I no longer had the strength to mourn for her.

I wasn't hungry but my body felt as if it weighed a ton and I became weak and listless. Luckily, we didn't have to work. We were sitting or standing around aimlessly waiting for a decision about where we would be going, watching the sky for aircraft, hoping for bombs. I remember the heat, the identical concrete buildings, the watchtowers and the fence of electrified barbed wire. There was a railing around it to prevent prisoners from launching themselves against the high-voltage wire. People who had run against the fence to kill themselves in the past were called 'Musulmans' because their dead bodies, stuck to the wire; looked like Moslems in prayer.

It was some days (or weeks?) later that they lined us up, five abreast, for an unknown destination. We shuffled ahead for so long that we seemed to move in a circle. The barren landscape of identical roads under the blazing sun made me dizzy. Where were they taking us? Was it to different showers? They said that the gas chambers had showers to fool those who were destined to die. 'We're being taken to be killed,' said one part of my brain to the rest, which refused to believe it. The sun shone relentlessly, time ceased to exist. After a long time, the column came to a standstill. We seemed to have arrived. People stopped talking to each other and the droning of distant aircraft became stronger. Then, defying orders, they began to sit on the concrete pavement. I sat down too. There was nothing left but the blazing sun, the showers with their gas pipes, and the solace of my own body

Anger and pity should not come into this narrative, but the memory of women in agonised fear openly masturbating on the road is not easy to bear. Much later, in England, I saw a retarded baby who had been abandoned in a park. The nurses complained that they could not dress her because she kept tearing off her clothes in order to hold her naked body tightly with both arms.

It was not the gas chamber after all. People in the front sent word back that we were being registered. The column began to move and people got up. When we turned a corner I saw women in uniform sitting at a table by the roadside. One of them was asking for names and dates of birth which she entered in a book, another stamped a number on outstretched arms. I was almost there when the sirens began to wail because of an air-raid. Some of the guards ran for shelter. The column went into disarray and when it was reassembled, I found myself among those who had already been stamped.

That is why I have no number on my forearm. It had no practical consequence in the camps, but at the time it meant a great deal for me. I was convinced that after the war the Germans would never allow people, branded like cattle, to bear witness and thought that without a number on my forearm I had a hope of survival.

2

The fact that I did survive was due to luck as well as to acts of goodwill. There was, for instance, the young doctor in the Studhof camp whose name I never knew.

The transfer to Studhof at the end of August was unexpected but the train journey was nothing like the cattle wagon which brought me to Auschwitz. It was an ordinary coach with seats and windows which could be opened, but it was, as always, filled with more people than the number of seats or even the standing room. I curled up under people's feet on the dirty floor desperately trying not to mind the bucket which splashed urine over me whenever the train jolted. 'I can bear it, I can bear it,' I chanted to myself all the way, so as not to become hysterical. (Later, when I told my analyst about that endurance test, she was not impressed. Endurance was all very well, she said, but you should be careful not to make it a strategy for life). Moving us to Studhof near the North Sea seemed to have no purpose. It was similar to Camp Birkenau in Auschwitz, except that instead of concrete there was sand under our feet. I could smell the sea which I'd never seen. By this time, I was desperately hungry because my bowels had begun to function once more. In addition to the hunger gnawing at my insides, an abscess had developed in my right ear

The memory of past emotions can be evoked at will, but the memory of physical pain is like an empty shell. I only remember that I was crouching on the ground, crying with pain while I poured sand, baked by the sun, into my ear to ease it. I must have been in agony because somebody persuaded a doctor to see me. The doctor was reluctant to leave the spot near the kitchen where her shaven head was not exposed to the sun and where she could talk to the kitchen staff, but she finally agreed. She looked into my ear and said that the abscess should be opened up to prevent it from spreading inwards.

'It hurts terribly,' I sobbed.

'What do you expect me to do about it?' she asked angrily, 'You don't imagine someone will give you an aspirin, do you?

'My gums are bleeding too. And look at my nails, they're sore.'

'It's the scurvy,' she said. 'Vitamin deficiency. Sailors used to have it on the open sea. As for your ear, you can pray that is will burst. If not...'

She turned round and left me. She returned an hour later with an onion and a piece of carrot hidden under her prison shift.

'I managed to get this from the kitchen. Don't let anybody see it,' she said.

A raw onion was bliss. Somehow I managed to lick and chew the carrot too and almost immediately my gums stopped bleeding. Hot sand in my ear must have helped because the abscess suddenly burst. It was with tears of gratitude that I grabbed up handfuls of sand to clean away the pus pouring from my ear.

We were packed into a train once more; then we walked, and it was on foot that we arrived at our final destination, a camp in a forest in Poland. The campsite was ready for us, with circular plywood huts, kitchen buildings and living quarters for the guards. The Camp Commandant, a man in his fifties in S.S. uniform, made a sort of welcoming speech promising good treatment if we worked hard. The huts held sixty people, each with a spokeswoman or 'elder' to translate orders. He asked for volunteers who could speak German. I put up my hand but he chose Gerda, a German woman who had fled to Hungary some years ago to escape deportation.

The huts had no windows and only one door. Fresh straw had been strewn around the inner wall to sleep on and there was a stove in the middle with its pipe sticking out from the roof ready for winter. Each of us received two blankets and a spoon and a metal bowl with which to queue for food. Next day, we started digging a trench, about two miles away from the camp. It was to be a tank-trap to prevent enemy troops advancing towards Germany from the east. There was no sign of a gas chamber, and we had more and better food than previously.

'It's a holiday,' said Klari, a young woman I had befriended on the way to the camp, 'Have you noticed that he didn't say anything about punishment?'

The air was fragrant with the smell of pine, the huts were neat and clean, and the fact that the Camp Commandant talked in an educated German seemed more significant to me than the SS uniform he was wearing.

I was willing to work sufficiently hard that I might even be rewarded with something like a double ration of bread. It was a place to inspire hope.

I found a place on the straw but, to my regret, it was not next to Klari who settled down near her friend Ruth. Next day, we went to work escorted by brutish young Lithuanian guards who had very little German and used the butt of their rifles to make themselves understood. According to the Camp Commandant our food ratio was calculated for prisoners doing heavy work, the highest number of calories a female could get. It was distributed once a day after work and consisted of a bowl of soup, a chunk of grey bread and a dollop of margarine, which was sometimes supplemented by a spoonful of solid sweet jelly. It was more than we had before, but the calories were not calculated for survival. After a while people became weak, complained of pain and diarrhea, and ended up in the sick-bay, from which there was practically no return.

The hut had become half-empty by the end of Autumn, so that space was no longer a problem. The straw on the floor had rotted into a soggy mess and we discovered that it was better to sleep in pairs, spreading two of the thin blankets on the floor and two on top. As winter advanced we became expert at not turning in our sleep, except by agreement.

The Whip - a story.

In a clearing in the forest, not far from the camp, two soldiers were rolling to and fro on the ground locked in a fight. Their faces were flushed and their breath was like white mist in the cold air. Anton was kneeling over Marek, whom he had pinned to the ground.

'Had enough?' he asked.

Marek spat out a mouthful of snow as he scrambled up, brushing the snow from his trousers. He was a stocky boy of eighteen with fair hair and a round open face. His shoulders were broad but he was short, having barely reached the regulation height for the German Army. Although the fight was half in jest, he felt humiliated.

'You tripped me over,' he said angrily, 'You did it on purpose.'

Anton was putting on his anorak, panting and triumphant.

'So what? Hurry up, we must go back. Sarge will want to know where we've been all this time.'

Marek kicked hard at the fir-tree towering above him. 'I'm not afraid of him. Nor of you. I'll show you next time, see if I won't.'

Anton did not answer. They stood irresolute, reluctant to leave.

'You had a letter this morning,' said Anton, 'Do you want me to read it out for you?'

Marek's face turned scarlet, 'I can read!'

'Of course you can. Now give me the letter.'

Marek brought out an envelope from his inner pocket. He carefully took out a folded page torn from a copybook, and handed it to Anton.

Anton wiped his hand before he took the letter. He began to read it aloud.

'Dear son,' he read, 'I hope that this finds you in good health as we are but for Granddad's legs. Your auntie Bosi is expecting again but with God's help she will manage. We had to slaughter the pig because...' Here Anton stopped. Nearly half the letter had been crossed out with the heavy black ink of the censor. Then he continued. '...managed to send you a parcel which you should get before Christmas. Granddad wants me to tell you to be obedient and do as you are told because you are very lucky to be at the posting where you are. I pray to the Virgin Mary every day that they don't move you to another post somewhere else. For which I thank God. I hope that you are in good health and contented. Your loving mother, Zofia Kuderka.'

Anton returned the letter and spat on the ground.

'Good posting,' he said,` I could be with the Wehrmacht if that bloody doctor hadn't made a fuss about my finger. They thought that with a crooked finger I was no good for anything but this rotten place.' He dug his hand in his pocket and yelled at Marek in a sudden anger.

'Say something you dumb bastard, don't just stand there and grin!'

Marek's empty smile froze into a mask. As always when he was called dumb his fist jerked into action. But Anton didn't want to fight any more. He turned round to go back.

Marek put the letter back in his pocket and followed him in mute frustration. It was true that he could not put into words what was wrong with his posting. In the fifth year of the war they were lucky to be far away from the front. There was no fighting and no hard work to do. The food ration was generous and there was plenty of wood to keep them warm in the barracks. It was better than freezing to death in Russia. His mother was right; he ought to be grateful.

Marek, like most of the others, came from Lithuania. He could barely remember life before the war. It was better not to think about the freezing winter mornings on the farm, the long journeys on foot to the school, the dunce's hat and the teacher's leather belt. He did not want to think of his father either.

'Speak up, you idiot! Why am I cursed with a halfwit for a son?

But he had stopped shouting when the men with rifles came and took him away because of the grain hidden in the cellar. He was trembling and looked pitifully weak when they led him out of the house. Marek's mother stood crying and wringing her hands but Marek knew that he'd done the right thing. Loyalty to the Führer overruled duty towards one's father.

It was in the Hitler Jugend that his real life had begun. He was good at obeying orders and standing to attention with unblinking eyes, even when he was punished. The lads were ordered not to tease him when he stammered or could not remember the words of the oath. The Führer had changed his life. 'For all I am and all I have, I thank you, our Führer,' as the song said. He had hardly dared hope to be accepted into the army, but this year they had started to enlist his age group for special assignments, and had taken him on

Guarding the prisoners was easy, much easier than looking after the cattle at home. The food was good and there was plenty of it. And yet, whatever his mother wrote in her letter, this was a rotten place. Marek spat on the ground.

A large section of the forest had been cleared for a tank trap. It consisted of a trench, 6 feet deep and very wide, in which hundreds of women were working, digging out stubborn roots from the frozen soil with their spades. Some were shovelling the soil from the ditch, others were carrying the debris in a wheelbarrow to the rampart. Their shaven heads and emaciated faces gave them a weird similarity to puppets in a marionette show. They moved sluggishly so that from a distance they seemed not to be moving at all.

The guards stood scattered in small groups near the trench, smoking and chatting, waiting for the end of the day. Anton joined the others, but Marek did not go with him. He sat down on a tree trunk, feeling angry and frustrated. The constant noise from the trench was so familiar that he hardly heard it. The creatures were forever shrieking and chattering in their weird lingo. He looked enviously at the group which Anton had joined. Anton was telling them something and threw up his hands in mock despair, and they all laughed. Was he talking about him? He could have taught the bastard a lesson if he hadn't tripped him over.

He took a cigarette from a crumpled packet. Smoking was forbidden, and in any case he hated it, but everybody smoked and he needed practice. The bitter taste in his mouth filled him with disgust.

Down in the trench, two women were loading a wheelbarrow.

They wore men's overcoats stamped on the back with a red Jewish star.

'What exactly do you mean by "their usual cunning"?' Klari, the older one asked the girl she was working with, 'Do you mean they're inherently cunning or that they respond with cunning to given situations?'

'I can't follow you when you talk like this,' the girl complained, 'You know what I mean. That gang of Slovaks talk Yiddish to their kind in the kitchen and get all the potatoes in the soup, so that what is left for the rest of us is water. Look at them,' she pointed at a group working at some distance, 'How is it that most of them have boots rather than clogs? They always get what is best yet most of them can hardly read and write.' She looked at Klari and wished she had not spoken.

'You stupid little fool. Do you think that you're superior because they speak Yiddish? So did your grandfather. Or great-grandfather,' she amended when the girl wanted to protest, 'The Slovaks have survived because they protect each other. They were starving in Auschwitz while you were practising the piano in your drawing room in Budapest.'

Anger made Klari short of breath but she continued, 'They despise us and rightly so. You should be ashamed of...' the rest was lost in convulsive coughing.

The girl was contrite. 'Please don't! You're right. I didn't mean it.' She was willing to say anything to mollify the older woman.

Klari still could not speak. A thin line of blood was running from one side of her mouth. She wiped it off with her dirty hand while she put her arm round the girl's shoulder for support.

'Get moving you two! Do you think I'll do your stint for you?'

Paula was kneeling in the mud behind them, trying to pull out a root with her bare hands. Her voice was hoarse with anger.

'Standing there chatting as if you were on a promenade! We shall never get finished because of the likes of you!'

They did not answer. Paula attacked everybody all the time, but if you as much as answered her, she burst into tears.

A few yards behind them Magda was talking to herself in a loud voice, reciting a recipe for stuffed carp.

'First soak the walnuts in milk, then add them to the grated carrots. No need to chop the onion finely because...'

'Shut up! I can't bear your bloody cooking all the time. Nobody's interested in your recipes!'

'Shut up yourself, you bloody bitch. Leave Magda alone. I'd rather listen to her than to your boasting.'

'Who's boasting? I never boasted in my life. You're a liar. And where did this spoon come from anyway? Everybody knows you're a thief!'

The diggers glared at each other like sparring skeletons. Suddenly everybody was shouting, except Magda who went on solemnly about the stuffed carp.

Klari had recovered from her attack of coughing and was now ready to push the wheelbarrow towards the rampart.

'I'm sorry, I shouldn't have shouted at you,' she apologised to her friend, 'especially after your ordeal. Does your back hurt?'

'I told you. I didn't feel a thing when they hit me because I had my blanket wrapped around me.'

'The guards could have killed you. I still don't understand how you dared.'

'Neither do I. I fell back on the way here and one of the animals pushed me into a puddle.'

'The others said that you jumped up and attacked him.'

'I wasn't thinking. I only knew that my coat would never dry out and I shoved my spade into his belly. And you know what? He was frightened. The bloody bastard with his gun was frightened. He shouted to the others for help.'

'They could have shot you on the spot!'

'I know. I still don't understand how I did it. Two of them whipped me until I fell down again, then they let me get up and join the others. But you should have seen his face! He was scared; he was really scared.'

The girl started to laugh shakily and couldn't stop. 'You should have seen him! He looked like a startled ox!'

She wiped her tears with the back of her hand. Her sore back hurt but it was better than being shot. Anyhow, it was over. She picked up her spade from the ground.

'Let's get on with it, shall we?'

A whip wasn't exactly a regulation weapon but it was good for the image. The guards preferred birch twigs which they peeled and twisted into a plait. The techniques varied. Some believed in soaking the birch first, others thought that soaking took the bite out of it. Making and comparing whips was the latest craze in the barracks.

The thought cheered Marek up. On his last outing to the village he had bartered some army tins for strips of black leather. They were long and beautifully dyed, perfect for a whip. He had been working on the handle for days in secret, whittling away the bark from a piece of wood and carving a pattern in it with his penknife. It was a nice pattern, similar to the carving on the eaves at home. He could do anything as long as nobody was looking over his shoulder.

He took out the strips of leather from his pocket and began to plait them. The mist which clung to the forest in the morning had lifted and a friendly winter sun began to warm his cheek as he worked. He thought of outdoing the others and began to whistle. Frowning with concentration, he whistled a tune he had learned long ago.

'Little Hans – walks alone – in the forest all alone.' Or was it 'is not frightened on his own?' Plaiting the leather reminded him of the thick long hair of the girl with whom he used to play forbidden games in the loft. If only there were girls around here! Girls with strong arms, soft skin and round bosoms. Women with buttocks like melons when they bent forward at hoeing.

He glanced towards the trench. These creatures were not women at all. They were filthy and ridden with lice, and would stare at you uncomprehendingly when you said something. They were, of course, an inferior race. The Führer was right when he did not wish them to pollute the Reich.

He sighed, stood up and stretched, then strolled slowly to the edge of the trench. The prisoners had to be speeded up or they would idle the day away.

'Watch,' Marek said to a man next to him. He swished his whip and caught a woman who stood leaning on her spade. She screamed and stumbled. The others began to move towards her like ants do, when somebody throws a stick on the heap.

Marek beamed with pride as he tried the whip again. This time he hit one near the other side of the trench.

'I bet you couldn't make one like this in ten years,' he said. His round young face radiated pride when he handed the whip to the other man.

'You try it,' he said generously.

3

The hut 'elders' went to the office to receive the Camp Commandant's orders every week. Once, I had to deputise for Gerda, who had hurt her leg, and saw him at close quarters. He sat behind a desk facing the group of ragged women and looked so sick that one could almost forget that he had powers of life and death. He informed us that typhoid fever had broken out in the camp.

'I don't think you understand what this means,' he said, 'I've seen it happen before and I can tell you that if it's allowed to spread, no-one will survive. I have to introduce harsh measures in order to save the camp.'

The 'harsh measures' were the shooting of the sick and dying, so that they would not spread the disease. He wanted the hut 'elders' to report anyone they suspected of being ill. 'There is no other way. If you hesitate, you'll die,' he repeated. I saw, with some satisfaction, that he was scared.

The possibility of obeying the camp Commandant didn't even cross my mind. He was almost begging us to cooperate because he must have known that he would not be obeyed. As it turned out he was mistaken. The rapidly increasing death toll was, in fact, due to starvation. Had typhoid broken out among such starving inmates, the whole camp would have perished, including the guards. It was a miracle that no outbreak of a contagious disease occurred, since the camp was riddled with lice. We had neither underwear nor any facilities for washing, and we wore the same prison shift under whatever overcoat we had inherited from the dead. Hunger and cold were no longer acute sensations. I never heard anyone say that they were hungry. I lost so much weight that the skin covering my shoulder blades and hip bones became sore from contact with the ground on which I slept. Blood and pus were constantly seeping from my wounds because the sores and lesions would not heal. A bruised knee or chafed shoulder-blade remained in the same condition for months so that my body was covered with festering sores. On rainy days, or when the snow came, we went to sleep in wet clothes which did not dry before they got wet again.

What I was unable to tolerate was the lice. At first I tried to fight them, making an arrangement with the girl on night duty to wake me up to wash myself at the pump in the middle of the night when there was no thirsty queue in front of it. Sometimes, I had to break off the icicles to get the pump going before I stripped to the waist in the hope that the water would keep down the lice. I was the only one in the hut who forced herself to do this, but it made no difference; the lice were multiplying with frightening speed. When I noticed that they were feasting on my wounds, I snapped. It was not pain or hunger which finally got me, but revulsion. I no longer wanted to live. How could I bear what was unbearable? I was being eaten alive.

I was saved by a mobile disinfecting unit brought in from the front. It was a train with a steam engine and four coaches standing on a disused branch line off the camp, manned by four people wearing the uniform of the Wehrmacht. The prisoners were escorted to it in small groups. In the first coach, we were to strip naked while our clothes underwent a sort of dry cleaning by steam. We were then to walk to the next coach to take a shower, and then wait until our clothes were returned to us. The coaches were well heated and it was a great relief to put on disinfected clothes before returning to the camp.

I was chosen as an usher because I could translate instructions. My job was to get there first, strip, then lead the groups through the coaches. The men operating the unit were elderly Germans, whose horror was almost comical when they first saw the naked skeletons invading their train. I translated their instructions, walking with them from coach to coach, until they took a break, telling me to go with them to their living quarters in the last coach. There was a table in it and chairs and I was told to sit down. There was coffee bubbling on a small spirit stove and they produced some biscuits from a tin.

I looked around in a daze. Chairs, cups and saucers, knives and forks belonged to a different existence and so did questions like: 'Would you like some more?' They gave me biscuits and bread and margarine and talked openly about Germany losing the war. They showed me snapshots of their families and I understood that they were worried about their wives and children. In reply to their questions, I explained that I'd learnt German in the grammar school which seemed to surprise them. 'We did French too,' I said, 'and Latin.' They tut-tutted and asked me questions about where I came from, which induced me to show off even more. To prove that I could do better than speak rather basic German, I put my empty mug on the table and, stark naked, began to recite Goethe to them:

> ***'Wer reitet so spät durch Nacht und Wind***
> ***Es ist der Vater mit seinem kind...'***

4

It was dark in the hut when I wriggled from under the blanket I shared with Katinka and began to wrap a strip of material around my feet. The question whether to remove one's boots for the night was a matter of endless debate. It was certainly better not to have to search for them in the morning when the guards kicked the door open, but taking them off gave you the feeling that you'd undressed for the night. I had taken mine off a few hours before, when I had gone outside to wash myself.

Those nightly outings were good. The campsite was always deserted in the small hours of the morning. With the floodlights switched off, I could see the black outline of the forest against the sky. The cold air was clean and sweet to breathe and on clear nights I could see the stars. It was a consolation to know that the stars, unmoved by human suffering, would be there until the end of time. The forest and the sky enfolded me in their immensity and I was reluctant to return to the hut where the darkness was alive with groans of pain and nightmare.

I shifted on the straw to examine my feet which showed no sign of frostbite. I was lucky to have a coat with a lining which could be torn into strips, because frostbite was a killer. Those who were unable to make the daily journey to the digging were finished.

I had a curious dream that night. Somebody, I could not remember who, had said: 'The war will end in December...' But December had gone by. Was it January? The weeks melted into each other. There was no day of rest to divide them. The cycle of twenty-eight days did not measure the time either because everyone stopped menstruating in the camps. Yes, it must be January, I thought.

'The war will end in December.' Everybody said that the Germans were retreating. French prisoners working in the forest would occasionally shout the latest news to us, or drop a page torn from a newspaper to be picked up, but the end of the war did not seem good news to me. Surely the Germans would not let the witnesses go free? Win or lose, they would surely eradicate every trace of the camps before a peace treaty was signed. I had no desire to think about what might happen to us when the war ended.

Katinka, with whom I shared my blanket, sat up next to me. 'My back hurts,' she wailed, but no-one took any notice. She was a tall child of barely fourteen who had got separated from her family on arrival at Auschwitz. She had discovered a distant relative in the camp whom she called her aunty, and to whom she stuck like a limpet. When her aunt had died, a few weeks previously, I had offered to share blankets with her, partly out of pity, partly because she was a sound sleeper. Of course her back hurt, so did everyone else's. The sores on our spines, hipbones and shoulder blades would not heal.

People began to stir in the dark and the hut became noisy with moans and arguments. The red glow of the small stove cast flickering shadows on ghosts moving around, or sitting on the straw to pick the fresh re-infestation of lice from their clothes

'Inferno,' said Klari, as she disentangled herself from the blankets she shared with Ruth, 'Can't you stop that girl snivelling?' she demanded, but I was getting up to listen to Gerda.

'Something is up,' Gerda said, 'the guards have been whispering among themselves for days. The kitchen girls said they were preparing double rations for tomorrow.'

'I heard it as well,' someone agreed, 'Have you noticed how thick the soup was yesterday? And the bread was much bigger than usual. They say we're going to get double margarine today. Why are they doing this? And where are the guards? Will there be no roll-call today?'

The door was thrown open suddenly, and the Camp Commandant entered, flanked by two guards. He was tall and had to bend his head to get through the door. The guards went around, shouting: 'Heraus! Everybody out! Los! Los! Out of the hut!'

There was no need to tell us to take our belongings. No-one would dream of leaving anything behind, because it would be stolen. We did not own much: Nina owned a needle which she would rent out for a quarter of bread, Vali, a bottle of aspirin from the sick-bay, and I treasured half a packet of cigarettes which a local man had thrown towards me outside the camp. A cigarette was worth a whole bowl of soup although I never understood how people could make such an exchange. I tied my bowl and spoon around my waist and looked for Katinka who was heading for the door.

It was still dark outside, a clear and frosty night, but the stars were beginning to fade. Everyone was out of the huts, only the sick-bay was still occupied. I shivered in the cold while the guards arranged us in rows of five. I glanced towards the kitchen, the way to it seemed free. Perhaps I could run and find a potato or two on the ground? But I was chased back and, in the confusion, I lost my place. I found myself next to people from other huts. The interpreters were called to the camp office but by the time they returned everyone understood that we were leaving the camp. We would be given food to last several days. Each person's ability to walk would be tested because the march would be long and hard. Those who were unable to walk would stay behind and be looked after.

The testing was simple. We had to walk, one by one, in front of a man in SS uniform. Those who limped were ordered to take off their boots for inspection. If their feet were sore with frostbite, they were told to stand aside. Anyone who felt she was unable to make the journey was allowed to join them voluntarily, and I saw, in horror, that Katinka was about to do so. 'Stay where you are, you fool,' I hissed, but I don't think she heard me. Anni, who was fighting her sister Eva all the time, was found to be unfit, and her sister joined her voluntarily. I didn't see Klari and, for a dreadful moment, I thought that she'd decided to stay behind. Did she not remember Auschwitz? Then I saw her. Klari and Ruth – always Ruth! – were already in the queue which was moving towards the gate.

When it was my turn to be tested, I walked as if on parade hitting the ground firmly with my feet. Anyone could see that I had no frost bite. I joined the others without looking at those who were to be left behind. Near the gate a trestle table was heaped with mountains of bread, and buckets with jam and margarine. Two of the kitchen girls, supervised by guards, handed out the food. I could not believe my eyes. A whole loaf of bread, four times our daily ration, a chunk of margarine and a huge dollop of jam in my bowl! I began to eat at once.

We moved slowly ahead. We left the gate, turned into a lane which had been out of bounds before, then right again, skirting the camp. By now it was daylight, but the sky clouded over and a light rain had begun to fall. I did not look at the people next to me, did not care where we were going, nothing existed except the bread. Thinking had stopped, my senses went dumb. Bite, chew, swallow. Bite, chew, swallow. At first I tried to stop myself because we had been told that the bread had to last for several days, but the effort was too much. I fell on the bread again, scooping the margarine out of the bowl with my hand.

Those in the front stopped suddenly and the others stumbled against them. A shiver went through the column. The girl next to me grabbed my arm.

'Listen! Can you hear it?'

The barking of machine guns came unmistakably from the camp. I struggled against understanding what this meant. Women began to sob.

The guards, who knew the fate of those left behind, jumped into action prodding the prisoners with their guns. 'Los! Los! Move!' Somebody in front of me began to chant in a choking voice the prayer for the dead:

> ***'Yishkadal v'yishkadash shema...'***

5

I cannot remember now how long this march lasted. Was it three days, or perhaps four? No, it could not have been four days. I could not have survived that long. We spent nights in abandoned schools, in disused barns and finally in a prison, which had been evacuated before we arrived. During the day, we walked along the highway, followed by slowly-moving jeeps in which the guards took it in turn to get a lift. For us, there was no respite. Those who collapsed on the road were shot, their bodies pushed into the ditch.

My memory wanders like a searchlight in the dark, but illuminates only a few fragmented scenes. These keep shifting back and forth, so that it's difficult to put them into any kind of sequence.

I see a yard behind a large building where the guards have slaughtered a pig which they are about to roast on a makeshift fire. One of them throws a piece of fat towards me. I catch it and begin to eat, tearing at it with my teeth and nails because others are already running towards me.

In another fragment, we have just arrived at a barn in a deserted farm where we are to spend the night. Everyone is running towards the water pump in the yard but I only want to get inside and lie down. The building smells of hay and animals and feels blissfully warm. I stretch out on the beaten earth, but the others are trying to do the same, so we get in each other's way. Somebody elbows my head away, while somebody else tries to put her feet on mine. We push and curse while more people, prodded by the guards, try to get inside.

Experienced soldiers, however tired, would probably have had the sense to fill the rear of the barn first, allowing room for the rest. They would have had the foresight to leave a lane between the prone bodies for those who wanted to go outside during the night. We just collapsed as soon as we got in. I barely had the strength to move my boots and put them under my head before closing my eyes.

The shouting and arguing eventually subsided and I fell asleep. It must have been nearly dawn when I was wakened by a wailing in the dark. 'Water, water, water…' a weak voice repeated with maddening monotony like a tap dripping. Can't somebody shut her up? I tried to go back to sleep. 'Water, water…' Others around her were trying to silence her… 'Water, water, water…' She was probably ill or dying – and she never stopped.

I put on my boots and began the laborious journey out of the barn, stumbling against cursing and kicking bodies in the dark. I reach the pump, fill my bowl with water and return to the unknown woman with what I haven't spilt. She drinks the water in noisy gulps and mumbles something while I crawl back to my place. I have no strength left to take my boots off again and fall asleep at once.

I sit up with a jolt. Panic has broken out. People are jumping up from the ground screaming and heading towards the door. I can dimly see the reason, and my heart stops. A shapeless creature, clearly not human, is moving towards me in the darkness, like the embodiment of a nightmare. Its bulk seems enormous. It tramples on the sleepers who sit up in sudden horror, while others are trying to escape through the door, fighting whoever is in their way.

The guards were awake and shouting, ordering everybody back but when they saw the cause of the pandemonium, they fell over with laughter. The crazy women were frightened by a cow! The cow, who wanted nothing more than to return to the barn, was led away. Anyway, it was time to get up. It seemed that an order had arrived to speed up the march. Those who had fled into the yard in panic were now back, searching desperately for their boots in the dark. But there was no time for that, they were chased out of the barn to face the journey with only rags tied around their feet. None of them would make it. Thanks to the unknown woman, however, my boots were still on my feet.

In another scene, it is night and I'm sitting in the doorway of another barn, rocking a girl whose head is in my lap. I've been doing this for some time because, in her delirium, she believes that I am her mother. 'Hold me tight,' she moans and begins to talk incoherently, her face glowing with the fever. I am bending over her and suddenly realise that she is dying. The rattle in her throat...TB. Tuberculosis! I jump up in horror, pushing her away. She tries to grab my arm but I disentangle myself and move away, rejecting her in the moment of her death when she thinks that I am her mother. She will die the same night but I shall be given an extra lifetime to remember.

Daylight. The highway winds interminably between wintry fields and distant villages. The snow over the fields had thinned into a yellowish net and the trees in the distance stand naked against the grey horizon. The guards are speeding us up, sometimes compelling us to run. Time and time again we hear shots behind us but stagger ahead, trying not to look at each other.

The sight of prisoners driven by the Germans must have been familiar to the local people because there is a small group waiting for us at the roadside with a bucket of fresh water. The villagers probably have little food themselves, but they bring a few pieces of last year's turnips and carrots, which they distribute among those who reach them first.

Was it morning or afternoon when we came to the city? The highway changed into a tarmac road, easier to walk on. Will they give us a rest before we reach the inhabited area? Perhaps this was the place where they intended to take us. But it was no good turning to Klari for reassurance because she would not answer. Her lips were swollen and her sunken eyes beneath her spiky hair made her look helpless and menacing like a plucked bird of prey. I could not see Ruth anywhere.

We entered the city in disarray despite the efforts of the guards, who tried to turn the scattered stragglers into an orderly formation. The butts of their guns became useless. People dragged their feet as if walking in their sleep.

After a while there was a tram track under my feet. We were walking in the middle of a wide avenue with tall buildings and shop windows on either side. The traffic must have been diverted, but the pavement was lined with people who stood watching us. My brain registered for a brief moment a woman in a fur coat who briskly turned her small daughter around, burying the little girl's face into her lap. We were not a sight for a child. Even the adult faces were distorted with disgust and pity.

Then it was the highway again. It began to snow. Gerda in front of me slipped and fell but I couldn't help her. I knew from experience that people would grab at your coat when you bent down to help them and that once you had fallen it was almost impossible to get up. The ground was pulling one's body, as a magnetic field pulls metal.

But Gerda got up herself up and was walking again. Then the road ahead seemed to swell into a mountain and I knew that I could not go on for very much longer. The march could go on for ever and ever, the highway had no end.

I became aware that something unusual was going on behind me. Those at the back stepped aside to let a girl on a bicycle through who had ridden after us all the way from the town. She had no headscarf and the snow was settling on her short fair hair as, slowly and cleverly, she swerved her bicycle between the staggering women.

'The Russians are catching up with you. Don't give up! They are less than twenty kilometers back. They are coming nearer…'

She was already ahead of me but I could hear her clearly.

'Keep going. Ten kilometers. Don't give up.' The girl rode past the guards as if they did not exist.

'They will shoot her!' whispered Klari, suddenly alive again. But the girl on the bicycle swerved into a country lane and, in a moment, was out of sight.

The magnetic pull of the ground under my feet had eased. Others too had straightened up in a last effort to keep on their feet. The army of ragged skeletons came to life and managed to reach the town of Koronovo where the Russians liberated us next day.

I have tried all my life to recall the face of that girl but I cannot. I can only remember her fearless young voice and the snow which settled on her short fair hair.

6

We had no idea how close the Russians were behind us when we came to the small hillside town which was to be our last stop. The guards in the rear forced us to move on relentlessly as we struggled uphill through the deserted streets. There was a blackout and the misty rain wrapped the houses in unreality. It took me some time to realise that the place where we finally came to a halt was a deserted prison.

It was a two storey building with a cobbled courtyard in the middle where we were told to wait. Those still able to stand supported each other, swaying with exhaustion, while others collapsed on the wet cobblestones. Our fate was uncertain because the Nazis, whose discipline was falling to pieces, could take us no further. Some of the guards had abandoned their posts during the previous few hours, yet none of us had attempted to run away. The guards who remained still had guns.

The rumour started somewhere at the back of the yard, but it reached everyone within minutes. Since they couldn't take us any further, we would spend the night in the cells, but they would shoot us at dawn. How would they do it? The guards had only rifles with them. Would they bring in machine guns?

They were moving people upstairs, opening the cell doors for them. I found myself in a large cell with girls I knew only vaguely.To walk into a brick building was like entering a palace. It was dry inside and there were real beds. I looked around. There was an electric lamp dangling from the ceiling. All the beds had blankets and a pillow. In the middle of the cell was a table covered with a cloth for which two of the girls were already fighting. It was stupid. Did they not understand that this was the end? I went to the nearest bed and fell on it.

Some women were praying, others cried. Two girls were locked in an embrace under the blanket, wildly kissing each other. Did I hear shots outside or was I dreaming? The light went off and I began to see confused images. In the morning there would be water. I would stand under a waterfall with cold water splashing over me and drink and drink…

Then it was morning. The patch of grey sky visible across the barred window high up in the wall became lighter. When would they come? It seemed as if hours went by while we tried to make sense of the noises outside, but the walls were too thick. It must have been mid-morning when we heard the sound of running, and a key was turned in the lock. I sat up in bed. The door burst open. A man in a grey uniform was standing in the doorway flanked by two civilians.

'Frauen, ihr seit befreit. Wahrend der Nacht hat die Rote Armee die Stadt erobert.'

He turned round to go to the next cell. We didn't need a translator to understand that the Russians had occupied the town during the night. I saw somebody's face distorted in a scream and blacked out.

Much later somebody brought me water; then a young Russian soldier came with a bucket of reddish brown soup made of bran. It tasted better than anything I had ever eaten.

Freedom - a story.

It has been snowing during the night, covering the empty streets with an unbroken white carpet. A light wind disperses the smoke from the chimneys and shifts the snow on a roof which falls down with a heavy thud on one of the military tanks lining the street.

It is mid-morning but the town is deserted. If there is something unreal about the scene it is not the absence of people – a small town street can be temporarily empty of people, even in mid-morning, – but the absence of footprints in the snow. There has been a curfew since the previous day when the occupying forces moved into the town. Only troops are allowed out-of-doors but even these have vanished into shelters against the bitter cold.

A small figure emerges from around the corner clad in something which must once have been a heavy overcoat, but is now barely more than a rug. She walks in a strange way, slightly swaying, because the snow clings to her wooden clogs, making them into stilts. Despite the curfew, she is in no hurry but moves in a leisurely manner as if strolling along a promenade. The thread of her footprints connects her with the state prison, the gates of which the Red Army had thrown open the previous day.

She stops suddenly to stare at a tank with the insignia of the Soviet Union. The hammer and sickle are symbols of rebellion against the Nazis. They had been banned in her country but here they are boldly displayed on the tank. She walks slowly up to it and brushes the snow off the top with her sleeve, marvelling at the beauty of the enamel.

She is still standing there a few minutes later, slowly stroking the emblem with her bare hands as if it were warm and alive. A Russian soldier who has taken shelter under a doorway suddenly becomes aware of her. He rushes out yelling something and points his gun at her. The girl takes no notice. She hardly glances at him but continues to stroke the emblem rocking slowly on her heels.

The soldier is taken aback by her lack of reaction. He lowers his gun as he recognises the rug, the emaciated face and the closely cropped hair, crawling with lice. He says something in Russian but it no longer sounds menacing because he knows that the curfew does not relate to her. He points to a house further up the street. As she does not respond, he walks towards the house beckoning her to follow.

The soldier opens a heavy entrance door and they go up a flight of stairs. He pushes open the door of a flat which is not locked, signals to the girl to enter, then turns round and leaves. From his flow of words she has only understood one: 'niemetsky' – Germans.

She finds herself in a kitchen. It is nicely furnished and, if it were it not so cold, one would think that its inhabitants had left only moments ago. There is half finished dinner on the table, plates and glasses, a bowl of cold sauerkraut with a ladle stuck into it, half eaten slices of bread, a fork under a pool of salt from an overturned salt-cellar. There is an open bottle of wine on the table and some in the glasses. The chairs have been thrown back; one has fallen to the floor.

The girl shuffles to the table reaches out her arm and grabs a handful of sauerkraut from the bowl. She licks it but then lets it fall.

The snow under the soles of her clogs begins to melt, so that she is steadier as she crosses the kitchen into the living room. The room is in semi-darkness because one of the heavy plush curtains is pulled across the window, but she can see the dining table covered with an embroidered cloth, the stuffed armchairs and the stiff-backed dining chairs, one of them overturned. The door of a carved wardrobe is gaping open, clothes on the floor, a silver candlestick on top of them. A large grandfather clock ticks between the two windows.

She stands by the door, looking around in wonder. There is a sewing box on the floor, its contents spilled everywhere. She slides onto the floor, next to the box, and begins to examine the objects, one by one. A pair of scissors. Is there really such a thing as a pair of scissors? She opens and closes them like a small child who has never seen one. She lifts a reel of cotton and lets it roll; then she retrieves it. There is a darning egg, safety pins, pincushion, tape measure – objects from a forgotten world.

She sits on the floor, in a daze, playing with the contents of the sewing box, oblivious of time and place. A man from the neighbouring flat has heard the noise and opens the door cautiously to investigate.

A glance at the girl explains who she is and the man says something to her. This time it is in Polish which she still does not understand but she stands up obediently and follows the man who wants her to go into his flat.

Again it is a kitchen, spacious and well lit. The man motions her to stay where she is until he has brought in a high stool which he places in the middle of the kitchen as far away from the furniture as possible. He gestures her to sit down, carefully avoids touching her, and carves a large slice of bread, liberally spreading it with liver pâté. He hands it to the girl, who does not look at him, but licks the paste without biting into the bread. She is no longer able to eat, but realises she is very thirsty. She climbs off the stool and without a word leaves the kitchen to return to the other flat. The bottle of wine is still on the table. She drinks from the bottle, spilling some of the wine on her coat. There is another bottle on the sideboard which she puts under her arm and leaves the house.

It is snowing again in fat, soft, heavy flakes. She is no longer on her own in the street. A few others like her are walking towards the prison with bottles and loaves of bread under their arms. Others have just emerged from the building and are looking around in confusion, blinking snow flakes off their eyelashes.

The prison gates remain wide open since it was liberated last night. She stumbles over a cobblestone and steadies herself. The yard in front of her begins to contract and expand like an accordion. The prison buildings have receded a great distance but she manages to reach them. She sees an old billiard table on the corridor, hoists herself on it with great effort, forgetting the bottle. Lying on her back she watches the ceiling of the corridor slowly lower to enfold her in darkness and oblivion.

7

I did not know at the time that it was jaundice that made me indifferent to food in the kitchen of that German family. A few days before liberation the guards had slaughtered a pig and one of them had thrown a piece of raw fat towards me. I had devoured it at once although I knew that my starved body could not tolerate it. By the time we arrived at the prison, I had a high fever. I lay unconscious on the billiard table on which I had hoisted myself, but must have come round several times because I remember asking people who passed by for water. My voice must have been very low because they did not hear me.

It took some days for the Russians to supply us with passes and organise transport to the next railway station. By the time they lined us up in the prison yard for the journey homewards, I was on my feet once more. I think there were lorries waiting outside the gate but I never saw them because, as soon as I took a step forward, I fell. The queue moved slowly towards the gate. I got to my feet with great effort, tried to walk, and fell again.

One of the Russians, an officer, bent over me. His kindly middle aged face had tiny red veins on the cheek. He blinked shortsightedly as he peered in my face.

'Can't you walk?' he asked. His badly pronounced German seemed to come from a long distance. 'If you're ill, we'll get you to the hospital.'

It was not the face of a soldier; it was the face of a man. A husband, perhaps, or the father of a girl like me. I wanted to hold on to him with both arms.

'No! No hospital!' I cried, 'I know what it means. When you say hospital it means gas chamber!'

Some low cunning made me say this because I knew perfectly well where I was. I saw compassion and made use of it. 'Don't take me to the gas chamber!' I stammered, 'Look, I can walk!' I was only half conscious but I tried to stand up again and swayed. He caught me up in his arms. His face darkened with pity and indignation.

'We are Russians. We have no gas chambers,' he said, 'Come, let me help you.'

He, himself, carried me to his car and drove to a cottage hospital on the outskirts of the town. Several others had been brought there already, propped up against the wall, waiting to be carried to the loft. It had to be the loft because the last stages of starvation made people incontinent and the nursing staff had refused to touch us.

The loft was clean and airy and they found blankets for us to lie on. The nurses brought bowls of soup, which they put on the floor, hastily, while holding their nose with handkerchiefs. One of them looked as if she was about to be sick and ran out, slamming the wooden door behind her. She returned several times with more soup and mashed potatoes, but left immediately.

It was the next day, or perhaps the day after that, when the nuns arrived; four nuns, their bonnets crisp and clean and skirts rustling, as they lifted the weightless bodies from the floor to carry them downstairs. Their faces reflected nothing but friendly concern as they went briskly about their business, tut-tutting at the screams of pain when they peeled off clothes, caked with dirt and blood. Downstairs, a wooden bathtub awaited us, with bandages and disinfectants on the table.

Two of them carried hot water in a bucket. The third prepared the bandages, while an elderly nun washed us one-by-one in the tub. She handled everyone with great tenderness, even when they tried to fight her, because the soap and the disinfectant hurt them. None of the nuns showed disgust or revulsion at the sight of our naked bodies, although even the doctor who came to see to the wounds turned his head away for a moment.

A smiling nun ,who kept talking to me in Polish, pulled back the sheet from the freshly made bed. Did she know who we were?

'Do you know we are Jews,' I asked her in German, but she smiled and shook her head.

After handing us over to the regular nursing staff, the nuns departed the next day. I don't remember much about the weeks that followed, except my relentless fight for food with the nurses who, again and again, tried to explain that the sudden intake of too much food might kill me. One day, a man came from the Red Cross and asked if any of us would like to send a letter home. There was no regular mail service yet, but he promised that our letters would arrive. Arrive where? I wrote a few lines on a piece of paper he gave me, without daring to believe that my sister would still be at home to receive it. There was a festering sore on my back which needed fresh bandages every day. Doctors rarely visited us, apart from a surgeon who came to remove frozen toes which had become septic. After a while, I could wander around and discovered a stack of paperback romances in an annex. My German had improved considerably by the time I finished the lot. It took several weeks before I was discharged and could begin my journey home.

Trains were already running but without either tickets or timetables. One waited at the station for a crowded train heading south and climbed on the crowded roof. My immediate aim, each time, was to reach the next town, where the Red Cross would provide us with bread and soup, and arrange shelter in disused school buildings or empty houses. When there was no train, I walked along the highway in the company of temporary friends. I would casually thumb a Soviet jeep as if the sole purpose of the Red Army was to give me a lift.

There was little traffic on the roads. People gave way to Russian uniforms and those on bicycles swerved warily away from them. I would step into the middle of the road to halt a jeep, even when it was heading a convoy. Amazingly, the soldiers never got angry. The driver would stop and stare at me while I said 'khleba' in my best Russian, indicating I was hungry. He would dutifully reach under the seat to take out his own ration of bread and tinned meat to share with me, which was no more than I expected. The Russians had saved my life, so naturally they had to feed me. Later in Budapest, I heard horrendous tales about hordes of Russian soldiers raping women at gunpoint, but those I met in Poland were different. Only once did an officer suggest through an interpreter that we go behind a shed 'for sexual purposes.' He did not seem much put out, however, when I politely refused the offer.

Spring in Warsaw - a story.

There never was an April like the one in '45, the year when the war ended. Crocuses and buttercups spurted among the ruins and the chestnut trees were bursting with life, their buds growing by the hour.

They said later that, by the end of the war, Warsaw had been razed to the ground, which was not quite true. No town can be entirely razed to the ground. There was life among the rubble, and many of the burnt-out buildings were still standing. A missing front wall could transform a house into a theatre stage. The April sun moving between the clouds lit up the props: a shelf clinging to the wall, a lamp dangling on a piece of wire, a lidless piano grinning on top of the rubble.

In the old ambassadorial quarter, a number of houses remained habitable. They served as temporary accommodation for liberated prisoners of war on their way home. One of the houses was allocated to women released from the concentration camps. It was a rococo villa with a beautiful wrought iron gate and oval windows from which the furniture had been removed. We slept on mattresses on the inlaid parquet floor in empty rooms with a stuccoed ceiling and ornate marble fireplaces. The neighbouring houses were occupied by men, mostly former members of the Belgian and Italian resistance. The compound was out of bounds for local people, but we could come and go as we pleased.

By the time I reached Warsaw, the repatriation of liberated prisoners had become more organised. The civil authorities printed temporary passports and advised us to stay in the town until special trains arrived to take us home.

The garden around the villa was overgrown with tangled weeds and full of rubble but it stretched itself in the April air and began to breathe again. It was warm that April and there was music. It was a mystery how the Italians acquired fiddles and guitars when the rest of us would have sold our souls for a bar of soap, but somehow they did, and I can tell you that music made with stolen guitars can be very sweet.

There were about a dozen girls in the large room which, we thought, must have been a small ballroom before the war. Our preoccupation was with clothes. A pair of scissors and a needle and thread appeared from nowhere. Those who were clever with their hands were busy cutting up army sheets and blankets into shirts and blouses. I admired them with helpless envy until a Belgian ex-prisoner gave me a whole carton of cigarettes for doing his laundry and I exchanged the windfall for a skirt and a blouse.

Can you imagine the thrill of it? I was twenty and my body was slowly changing its skeletal frame into the shape of a slim girl. My new hair, in happy surprise, began to grow into curls, and the sores around my mouth had disappeared. I was dizzy with freedom; we all were. And with hunger, of course, because no amount of food was enough. We could have eaten up the world and drunk up the air. The evenings were full of laughter and whispers in the dark. Couples disappeared behind the ruins or walked out into the countryside. Eros had a heyday. I too was briefly and insincerely in love with an Italian boy who did not understand why I refused to make love with him. I clung to the virginity which had saved my life when Mengele in Auschwitz mistook me as pregnant, but I could not tell him this because I did not speak a word of Italian. I tried my pathetic Latin in the hope it was near enough to Italian. 'Amo libertatem,' I declared and he answered in the universal language of lovers by kissing me. He too knew a little German but we couldn't bring ourselves to utter words like 'Liebe' or 'Heimat'.

But it is of one particular evening I wish to tell. Someone got access to the music room of the neighbouring villa and we held a dance. There were feverish preparations; hairbrushes, combs, a lipstick, a bar of scented soap, went round between us. Each of us had got rid of her prison clothes by then. We bartered, borrowed, or stole something nice to put on. A bunch of men's unfinished trousers from a tailor's raided shop were particularly popular. I remember a giggling girl kneeling in front of another, sewing up the fly from which the buttons were still missing. Hairdos were no problem since our hair was only a few inches long, but the men seemed to like it. We had only a tiny hand mirror between us so we used each other's critical eye to reflect our fineries. Our praises were mutually generous.

The dance in the neighbouring villa started at dusk. There was a serviceable piano in the upstairs music room, good enough to drum out the easy waltzes and fox-trots of the day. Miraculously, there was even a little wine, half a mug for everyone, which was enough to make us drunk. Two Italians took turns at the piano, but we would probably have danced even without music. The scent of Spring came through the open window and brought with it whispers and suppressed laughter from the dark. I danced and danced until I had to slide down the wall with exhaustion. My Italian had left by then, but there were others, trying to kiss or slap bottoms according to the custom of their origins. Someone arrived with a harmonica and tried to teach us a Sicilian folk dance, amidst laughter and protest.

Suddenly the laughter stopped. We all stood still. The pianist jumped up and the harmonica became silent. Everybody froze. The hideous, familiar sound of an air-raid siren filled the room.

Somebody switched off the light and we ran to the window. It was not only sirens we heard, but loudspeakers and church bells too, as if all the bells of Warsaw had begun to ring out. We ran downstairs and out of the house, and met a jubilant procession with makeshift torches and banners. An old man, tears running down his face, shouted in Polish:

'Berlin has fallen!'

The ball was over. I joined the others in the square crowded with people who tried to out-shout the music from the loudspeaker. There was a crowd around a bonfire, burning German banners. Strangers shook hands and embraced each other, laughing and crying with joy. The Allied flag had finally been hoisted over the Reichstag.

The music and the shouting rose high above the town and mingled somewhere with the death cries and screams of agony in Berlin. They must have sounded like a cry for mercy in the empty sky.

8

I made the last leg of the journey home on my own, having left the others at the railway station. I could have waited for a better method of transport than a freight train carrying coal in open trucks, but when I heard that this one went as far as the Hungarian border, I became suddenly impatient. I climbed on top of a full wagon, shouting goodbye to the girls, who shouted back that I'd be sorry if it started to rain.

It was the end of July and the cloudless sky promised a hot day. I lay down and stretched myself luxuriously. The coal was no more uncomfortable than pebbles on a beach and the coal dust was of no concern to me. I hadn't had a proper wash for ages, and had long forgotten that it was possible to own another set of clothes. I took off my boots but kept them close to me in case a bad-tempered station master spotted me on the way and chased me off the train.

The driver had seen me climbing up, but had turned his head away. The Poles did not mind liberated prisoners cadging free rides home. They had become a nuisance, always wanting something: food, visas, accommodation in bombed out houses. The war was over; the sooner they went home the better. I had a temporary identification card, but nobody had yet asked for it. Those days I could, like the Queen of England, travel without ticket or money. A glance at my closely cropped hair was enough to provide me with free meals at Red Cross soup kitchens, as well as free rides.

I did not know the fate of my family. Everyone said that there was no point in returning home because the city had been bombed flat and that all the Jewish families had been deported. I still wonder whether this rumour was spread deliberately to steer people away from countries which were about to become satellites of the Soviet Union. Politicians play strange games.

The train was running relentlessly towards the south. I shut my eyes and tried to concentrate on something else. Think of food. Soup kitchens gave priority to former residents, which would be an advantage in Budapest. Wasn't this, after all, why I decided to return so suddenly? I would sprinkle bread thickly with sugar, as they do in Poland. It tastes almost like jam.

At home, my aunt used to make gallons of raspberry syrup for Uncle Marci's dispensary. No, let's not think of Aunt Helen's raspberry syrup. Let's think of soup, a plate of goulash with lots of meat in it.

I became aware of a sharp pain in my jaw. I hadn't had a toothache for a long time and I didn't remember that it could hurt so much. Soon my whole head was throbbing with the pain. The train was moving too fast for me to jump off, and didn't stop at any station. I stayed on top of the coal all day, crying black tears of misery while fingering my cheek which had begun to swell up like a balloon. The terrible pain crowded out every other thought.

At this point, my memory breaks up, like those early celluloid film reels, blurring the picture on the screen. I don't remember when the pain stopped in my swollen face. I must have been lying on a bench in a waiting room somewhere, before I changed to the train that crossed the Hungarian border.

Soon it arrived at Sárospatak, a small town, famous since the Reformation for its college of higher education. A woman with a headscarf, as worn by the orthodox, was walking up and down the platform with loaves of bread in her arms. 'Anyone from the camps? Anyone from the camps?' she shouted. I got off the train but it was not information she wanted but to present me with a crusty loaf, still warm from the oven. Suddenly everyone around me was speaking Hungarian. I felt what the partially deaf must feel when a hearing aid suddenly transforms meaningless sounds into sentences. A little boy trotting behind his mother on the platform shouted: 'Anyuka, várjál!' until his mother stopped him. I had not heard a child speaking in Hungarian for an eternity.

Ostracised Greeks running from the Agora cursed their countrymen in Greek; Huguenots on St. Bartholomew's night shouted in French, the Pilgrim Fathers took their language to America. The mother tongue is a good mother. People on the platform at Sárospatak station looked at me with hostility or indifference but the language they spoke welcomed me home.

The good woman looking for people from the camps was, with the help of American food parcels, running a soup kitchen in her home. I went with her to freshen myself up and have my fill of bread and a meaty soup.

On the next train to Budapest I found a seat by the window facing the engine. The train was full but the seat next to me remained unoccupied. People had learned during the war that lice were as contagious as the plague.

Now that the toothache had gone, I could no longer postpone speculating about the fate of my family. If my father had been taken to Auschwitz, he could not have survived. Could Aunt Helen and Uncle Marci have been spared? My sister, Marinka, and her daughter, Evi? I had seen what happened in Auschwitz to women with young children. If only three of them survived, who should it be? If only two – and what if only one? Who should it be? Who did I want it to be? I had been obsessed by this game of numbers since my liberation. Marinka? Evi? But if I wanted it to be Marinka, that meant the loss of the others. Choosing between them made me cringe with guilt, like a murderer.

The only way to get rid of this obsession was to accept that they were all dead. Total devastation is beyond grief. It created a limbo around me which the pain could not penetrate. It was, at the same time, a kind of freedom. Freedom from human ties, freedom from the responsibility of what I should do with my life. I had learnt on the way home what absolute freedom meant and I would not want any of it again. It was in this dream-like state that I had climbed onto the coal wagon, but now reality was rushing back to me like blood to a numbed limb.

I remembered the day when I returned from nursery school, crying, 'They've called me names! They said I was a carrot-head and ugly!' Marinka came running from the kitchen and picked me up as if I were a baby. She danced with me in the bedroom, turning me round and round until I was dizzy and stopped in from of the mirror.

Mirror, mirror on the wall,
Redheads are nicest of them all!

She used to call me her 'little chick' and filled my head with wondrous tales about the fairy Melusina who transformed the coal cellar into a marble palace when everyone was asleep. She invented a little brother of ours, who had died before I was born, and talked about him in a mournful voice which made me cry. My mother, amused and indignant, had quite a job persuading me that the little brother existed only in Marinka's imagination. But soon she would invent something else to frighten me or make me laugh. I was convinced that the fairy Melusina looked exactly like her.

Marinka would not have waited until they came to fetch her. When Leon provided Erika and me with fake identity card, I had persuaded him to do the same for her and her husband Dani. Did they take the risk? How could she hide under a false name with a little daughter? Dani was in a labour camp. She and her daughter made two, with Dani it was three. If only three of them had survived...

The train got nearer and nearer to Budapest. The game of numbers would soon become a reality. It was not too late to alight at the next station and to run back. I watched the distant hills sliding back to the frontier and tried to fight down my panic. The woman on the opposite seat got off noisily at a station, giving up her place to a fat man who sat fanning himself with a felt hat. He leaned forward with an alcoholic grin and tapped my knee.

'Going home at last, eh?'

I nodded.

'And where might that be? Budapest? I've seen many like you but they were mostly in groups. How come you're alone?'

He said that he was a commercial traveller going to Miskolc, a town some twenty miles ahead. He was going there on business, he emphasised, flashing a gold signet ring at me. His fingernails were dirty, and he smelt of rum, but he grinned at me in a friendly manner.

'Have you ever been to Miskolc?' he asked, 'It's improved since the Russkies came in. There's a nightclub where you can get anything, even American whisky if you have the right connections.' He winked at me.

'You get off with me in Miskolc and I'll take you to a pastry shop. You can have as many cakes as you like, and I'll pay for them. They've got cream cakes and cakes with sultanas in them – and chocolate. I bet you wouldn't refuse a chocolate cake, would you?' he said persuasively, 'I know a little hotel which is nice and clean and you could get on the next train to Budapest tomorrow. What do you say?' He leaned forward and leered at me with an expectant grin.

I felt my face going red with helpless fury. This fat slug, this filthy toad, knew that they'd starved me and thought that his time had come. I was filled with such loathing that it choked me. Had the other passengers heard him? Was there nobody who understood what he was proposing?

My rescuer did not come in shining armour but in a pair of slacks and a faded shirt. He was a young man who got up from his seat behind the commercial traveller and walked over, placing himself between us.

'May I present myself?' he asked, and told me his name. I looked at his outstretched hand before I realised that he wanted to shake hands with me. He said that he was a journalist, and could he have a word with me? The man opposite mumbled some obscenity, sank back on his seat and pulled his hat over his eyes.

'It's one of the concentration camps that you're returning from, isn't it?' he asked, and sat down next to me, 'I've been commissioned to write an article and have interviewed some people, but I need more material. You are a God-sent opportunity.' He opened his briefcase and took out a notebook. `We have at least two hours before arriving to Budapest. You don't mind talking to me, do you?'

'You're from Budapest,' I cried, `Do you know the area behind the Opera House?Has it been heavily bombed?'

'No idea, sorry. You see I live on the Buda side and only go to Pest to the newspaper office. At the moment, I am only freelance, but...'

`Do you know where Hajós Street is? The street between the Ring Road and the Opera House? Are the houses still there? You must know whether the Opera House has been bombed!'

He shrugged his shoulder. 'Not as far as I know. Not too badly, at any rate. Was this where you used to live?'

'At number twenty four, with my aunt and uncle. My sister Marinka lives in the next house, number twenty six. It's a modern building, easy to see from a distance,' I gabbled, 'You must know whether the area had been destroyed! And what about Damjanich Street? The big chemist shop? Everybody knows it. It's the largest chemist shop in the district. It belongs to my uncle.'

He looked unhappy, but there was little he could say. He shook his fountain pen to give it an even flow.

'Look here, shall we begin? There are stories about gas chambers and live electric wires, but they're not easy to believe. You must have suffered a great deal. Will you tell me about it?'

I thought about it. 'I had terrible toothache,' I said.

He sighed and put away his notebook. 'This is clearly not my day,' he said, 'but I can't force you if you'd rather not talk. To tell you the truth I came to Sárospatak partly in order to barter some meat, but I didn't have much luck with that either. Would you like an apple?'

'Tell me more about Budapest!' I begged him, 'What happened to the Jews?'

The picture was less bleak than I had expected, after Warsaw. Most of the Jews in the ghetto had survived. Some had survived deportation and were returning home.

Suddenly, it seemed that the train was hardly moving. What was I doing in Poland lingering in Red Cross shelters, using every opportunity to delay my return? I should have come home as soon as I was out of the hospital. Home to Aunt Helen, home to my Turkish bedspread, and the roll-top writing desk which had been a present for my fifteenth birthday. A minute ago, I wanted the train to slow down; now I was desperate for it to speed up.

I should have gone straight home. They'd probably be there, eating their hearts out for me. There was that man from the Red Cross who had come to the hospital in Poland and taken our names and I had even scribbled a letter, addressed to Aunt Helen. The news that I was alive could have reached them ages ago. My boyfriend was probably in Poland by now searching for me there. The rattle of the train slowly began to chant a promise.

The young man next to me had leant back on the seat and shut his eyes. He didn't open them until the train was pulling into the Eastern Terminal in Budapest. When people began to collect their baggage from the racks, he stood up and stretched himself with a yawn. He shook my hands and wished me all the best. Soon everybody had left the carriage and an old railway porter began to sweep the litter from the floor.

He must have told me to leave the train because it was on the platform that I was overtaken by blind panic. I must have lost my head completely.

I remember fighting a ticket collector who would not let me get back on the train once more. 'This is the terminal,' he kept saying, 'you can't go back. We've arrived at Budapest. Stop fighting me!'

'What's wrong with her?' somebody in the gathering crowd asked.

'Search me,' said the ticket collector, 'She must be mad. She says that she wants to go back, but we're not scheduled to return until tomorrow morning.'

'I'm not leaving,' I sobbed, 'There must be another train. Let me go!'

A policeman approached with measured steps. 'What's going on here?' he asked. Suddenly the journalist was beside me and linked his arm into mine.

'It is alright, officer. The girl is upset because she doesn't know about her family. I'll take her home. Please let us go!' He pushed aside people in the crowd and led me out into the street.

'Calm down,' he said, 'I'll walk you home to see what the score is. Should the worst come to the worst, I'll find you a place for the night, and we'll see where we go from there. Is it alright?'

I nodded gratefully and wiped my tears with my hand. The Ring Road in front of the terminal widens into a busy square, from which two avenues lead to the Danube. The scene in front of me was so brilliantly lit by the afternoon sun that I had to close my eyes. A loudspeaker was bellowing some military music and there were people everywhere, walking on the pavement, waiting at the crossing, going in and out of the shops. Two majestic trams came, dragging their yellow coaches behind like stately hens.

The tram could have taken us to the National Theatre, from where the number 6 goes to the Octagon, not far from the Opera House – instead of which we walked. My journalist friend turned into a side street, walking fast. It was clearly not the quickest way home, but I followed him meekly, speaking very little. I was not fit for conversation and he did not insist.

He turned the corner and stopped in front of a barber's shop.

'I need a haircut and a shave. You can wait for me outside. I won't be long,' he said. A bell attached to the door kept ringing until he closed the door behind him.

It's hard to believe it even now. How could he? He offered to put me up if my family had been wiped out, yet he went to a barber's shop and let me wait outside. How long does a haircut take? Half an hour? An eternity? I leant against the wall and stared at a makeshift fence in front of a bomb site.

At last, he emerged from the shop and said something about going to a party. We continued to walk towards Hajós Street. Some of the houses were burnt out, others were pockmarked by fallen plaster. The crossroads were as familiar to me as a mother's arms, but they didn't embrace me into a loving welcome. I pulled the anorak (which had been given me by a liberated Belgian prisoner for doing his laundry) closer around me.

Number 24, Hajós Street, my childhood home was there. So was the next-door house where my sister lived.

I left the journalist standing at the doorway and ran up the stairs. Tinted glass windows in the staircase. Wrought iron railing of the inner corridor. First door on the left. A notice pinned to the door with Aunt Helen's handwriting:

'Gone to No. 26 Hajós Street. Please leave the parcel with the janitor or bring it over.'

I flew down the stairs, shouting, 'They're alive!' at the young man, whom I never saw again. Up the stairs of the next house, three steps at a time. I threw myself against the door, kicking and hammering at it with my fists. I saw my sister's silhouette growing clearer against the opaque glass of the door as she came running towards me.

I fell into her arms sobbing and gasping for air. Aunt Helen was right behind her. 'Dani? Evi?' I asked when they let me go and I could speak again.

'They're alright,' my sister said, 'They are both alright. They just went to the corner shop and should be here any minute.'

'Uncle Marci?' I steadied the hand of my aunt who was unable to stop stroking me. A second of hesitation was enough for an answer.

'But there is still hope,' my sister said. 'If you came back, perhaps he too… You're back! You're alive! My little chick, look at me. What have they done to you?'

'Aunt Margit? Erika?'

'Margit is in hospital, but she's better.'

'And Erika?' I pushed my aunt away, 'She was only nineteen!' I shouted, 'She wasn't there when the Gestapo came for us. I thought she'd escaped!'

I did not have to ask about my father, who was sixty two when he was taken to Auschwitz.

Dies Irae - a story.

St Lőrinc was a dusty suburb on the Budapest-Cegléd highway. Its streets were choked with dust in the summer and became a sea of mud in autumn and spring. My mother hated it.

'Nandor is going to buy Aunt Helen a silver fox collar,' she told me when we were alone in the shop. She was wearing an old felt hat and two shabby cardigans on top of each other to protect her from the dust which settled on every surface and made her hair prematurely grey.

'I could have helped her choose the fur. All furriers are cheats and she wouldn't know the difference,' she declared, as if she were an expert in silver foxes. She looked out of the window towards the main road where a yellow streetcar had just arrived from Budapest and sighed, like a Roman matron on the wrong side of the Adriatic, separating her from civilised Rome.

Aunt Helen, my mother's younger sister, lived in Budapest with their rich brother Nandor who bought her nice dresses and went with her to expensive holiday resorts because it was important that when she married again it should be to the right man. To my sorrow, my mother had already been married when Uncle Nandor became rich. Uncle Nandor said that my father had no ambition. A man without ambition would never make enough money to buy his wife a silver fox stole.

My mother became aware of my presence. 'Pull up your stockings, will you? They're like an accordion. And your hair is a mess. What did you do with your kirby grips?'

She shook her head in despair. I must have been a sorry sight with my short red hair and freckles, not at all like the daughter she ought to have had.

My mother loved beautiful things. Books were expensive, but the magazines, brought every Friday by a little old woman in exchange for last week's bunch, were full of stories and photographs of beautiful ladies. They were a window on a world that was different from ours. It was a world of willowy ladies and elegant gentlemen, motor cars and yachts, holidays in Abbazia and Biarritz. Abbazia was on the coast of the Adriatic, so that my Aunt Helen, who had been there, had actually seen the sea. Ladies who went to Abbazia would wear silver fox capes to meet their secret lovers in the shadow of the park. The sound of the waves beating against the cliff would mingle with the distant music of the Casino and the air would be fragrant with the scent of cypresses...

I knew what cypresses were because we had an oil painting in my parents' bedroom which represented sunset in a park. The sky behind the cypresses was golden red, and the flowering bushes were tinged with orange. In the background there was a marble column embraced by climbing roses. It was in that park that my mother would have liked to live.

St Lőrinc was grey with dust and grime. My mother was in the shop all day serving customers who knew nothing about cypresses and marble columns and in the evening she was often too tired to talk.

'I am called la bella Tangolita,' she would sing to herself when she was in a good mood, but we both knew that she would never go to Abbazia to see the sea. Her beloved oleander tree in a tub which came to St Lőrinc in the furniture van did not survive the move, and the two rose bushes which she'd planted in the tiny porch wilted in the dusty heat.

People cannot live without beauty. When Moses went to talk to the Almighty, his people, bereft of his Visions, made themselves a golden calf. My aunt cherished her silver fox, my mother worshipped a china coffee set. It must have been a wedding present, too precious ever to be used. It was hand-painted, with tiny strawberries, whose leaves and tendrils encircled the cups and climbed up to the rim of the pot. My mother would lift the cups one by one to show me how thin they were. 'Like rose petals,' she would say. As she took the china set from the glass cabinet, she always smiled.

'I vividly remember the house in St Lőrinc,' I said to my friend Lilli, half a century later, on one of my regular visits to Budapest.

'I could step into the courtyard as easily as stepping onto a stage.'

'You mean that you've been coming back to Budapest every year for twenty years but you haven't ever been back to St. Lőrinc? I'll drive you there, if you like. I wouldn't mind seeing the place myself.'

'Surely, you don't imagine that the house is still there? I was nine when my aunt took me to live with her in Budapest.'

'But your father stayed there!'

'Until he was taken by the Nazis – which was nearly fifty years ago. The house can't possibly still be there.'

To our amazement, I was wrong. Half the street remained intact, on the edge of an industrial estate. My parents' house was still there, although everything around it had changed. Lili stopped her car outside the gate, and we got out. The cobbled yard, which separated the house from the shop, had changed into a thoroughfare, but the tiny front garden was there, with two thirsty rose bushes. I couldn't believe my eyes.

'Would you believe it? This is like a scene from a surrealist film. Even the Venetian blinds look the same. Over there was the stable for Villam who pulled the cart when my father went to buy hay to sell.'

'Let's ask if they would allow us to go inside and look round. They'll understand when you tell them that you used to live here as a child,' Lili said.

We rattled the bolt of the gate but nobody came. I looked round and saw an old man in slippers coming out of the house opposite. He shuffled towards us.

'Mr. Szabó is not in. They're both at work,' he said looking at us with suspicion. 'Can I help you?'

'It's not them we want,' said Lili, 'my friend used to live here when she was a child. Long ago,' she added unnecessarily.

'I left when I was nine,' I explained, 'but my father stayed here until... until the last year of the war.'

The old man stepped back to have a better look at me. 'I knew him. He went to Budapest to see his married daughter and never came back.'

'A fascist gang took him off the streetcar on his way home. He was killed in Auschwitz,' I said.

His face lit up.'I know who you are! You're his daughter. Your sister came here after the war more than once. It was... let me see...twenty or thirty years ago that I saw her. How is she?'

He was unshaven. His trousers were held up by braces over a singlet which did not cover the coarse hair on his chest. An old man, probably wakened from an afternoon nap.

'Don't you remember me? I am István, István Lukács! We used to play together, you and my sister Kati. She passed away last year.'

Lili was holding on to the fence for support. 'You mean that you recognise her after more than fifty years? It's not possible.'

He was grinning with pleasure, as if he'd passed a test. 'I knew at once who you were. Mind you, I don't know that I'd have recognised you if I'd seen you in the street. No offence meant,' he winked at Lili. Then he remembered his manners.

'You can't stand here in the street. It's no use waiting for the Szabós. Come with me, I'll call my wife. She'll be surprised!'

He went ahead to open the gate into a neglected garden where a few chickens raked the ground, supervised by a magnificent cockerel. He fetched two chairs from the porch and carried them to a rickety trestle table under an acacia tree.

'Take a seat. I'll call the wife and get something to drink. I'm afraid we haven't got any wine... never mind. You make yourselves comfortable. I won't be long.'

He shuffled into the house.'Mari! We have guests!'

A door was shut and we heard the muffled sounds of an argument.

'I would never have recognized him,' I said in a low voice to Lili, 'What on earth did we come to this house for?'

'It's obvious that he knows you. Mind you, he could have been guessing when you mentioned your father. Are you sure that you didn't come here after the war?'

'Oh yes,' I said,'Quite sure.'

When the war was over, and the fighting had stopped, my sister and her husband made the journey to St Lőrinc on foot, in the hope of getting news of my father. Bursts of machine guns could still be heard in the distance as they made their way, dodging overturned army jeeps and tram line tracks wrenched from the ground. When they got there they found that St Lőrinc was not as badly damaged as Budapest. My father's house was undamaged, but empty. The furniture had gone, as well as the bedding, the clothes, the rugs and curtains from the rooms, the pots and pans from the kitchen. Light switches had been torn from the walls and someone had even removed a window pane. Nothing but the bare walls remained.

It was more or less what they had expected. The family, to whom the house had been allocated as 'abandoned Jewish property' had fled, and hatred and poverty had done the rest. What they wanted to know was whether any of the neighbours had heard of my fate.

But the neighbours had been hostile. They didn't want to open their doors, and denied having seen or heard anything. 'Leave us alone!' one of them shouted at my sister. 'More Jews came back from Germany than went there, more's the pity!'

'There was nothing there,' my sister told me, 'not even a pencil or a pair of socks to prove that he'd ever existed. But he'd forgotten to take his cigarette case when he last visited Aunt Margit. I kept it for you.'

Blinded by tears, I put my inheritance into my handbag. No, I could not bring myself to go to St Lőrinc again.

'I hope you don't mind lemonade,' our host put a bottle on the table. 'Mari is making coffee. Here she is now.' A fat old woman emerged from the house carrying a tray. She wore a dirty white blouse with a faded skirt and had a gypsy scarf around her shoulder. She put down the tray and wiped her palms on her skirt before shaking hands with us.

'Nice to see you, I'm sure,' she mumbled, putting the mugs in front of us. She lifted the coffee pot 'How much sugar do you take?' she asked.

The spout of the pot was chipped. There was a crack on its side, but the hand-painted strawberries with their leaves and tendrils, encircling the fine china remained as fresh and tender as they had been in my mother's hand.

Part Three

OUR FATHER STALIN

1

So I was spared the worst, unlike those who limped back from the camps only to find their homes occupied by strangers. The returning Jews had, on the whole, not been welcome. They demanded to know who had been members of the murderous 'Arrow Cross', who had last seen their parents, where their belongings had gone. 'More of them came back than went away', muttered people who had to return 'abandoned' Jewish property to the owners.

The final battle between the departing Germans and the Red Army in January left much of the city in ruins. By the time I arrived home in August, the corpses of people and dead horses had been cleared away from the streets and the shops were open. Electricity was restored and the trams were running, but so many houses had been destroyed that sharing became compulsory. When Aunt Helen returned from hiding she found her flat occupied by refugees from Transylvania. She was allocated one room, sharing the kitchen and bathroom.

Uncle Marci, so proud of being regarded by his gentile friends as one of them, had, thank God, the strength to commit suicide. The 'real gentleman' with his silver cane-handle and butterfly tie had been sent to work as a chemist in a small town in the north. When the local Jews were rounded up for deportation, he made use of the poison to which he had access. It was a relief not to imagine him being pushed into the gutter by a grinning thug, or to think about the state of his kid gloves in the cattle truck.

It was his and Aunt Helen's former bedroom which I now occupied. As a teenager I used to sleep on a sofa bed in the living room, so I was delighted to have a room of my own, even if its only access was through the bathroom. There was a convertible bed in it and two chairs, remnants of the original furniture. If there was a wardrobe it must have been empty. The stacks of embroidered linen for my dowry had disappeared, together with Uncle Marci's fine wardrobe and Aunt Helen's fur coat and silver fox.

The word went round that I was home, and those of my friends who had not died or gone abroad came to see me. Eli Bohrer, whose photograph I had swallowed on my way to the Gestapo headquarters, was the first. My sister Marinka must have telephoned him because he came running to the door, almost immediately after my arrival. I ran into his arms, forgetting that my busy aunt had poured a mixture of garlic and vinegar on my head which she knew to be an infallible deterrent against lice. Its smell caused a sharp shock to enthusiastic visitors, but Eli didn't mind, he was in love with me. Why didn't I marry him? He was probably the nicest of those who had ever asked me. Retrospectively, I shake my head in disapproval, like a grandmother lamenting the loss of a good match. The answer, of course, is that I was not in love with him.

Imre Székely, my first boyfriend, who had rescued me at the dancing class and introduced me to Zionism, was dead. Unlike his mother, who waited day and night for his return, I had accepted, some time ago, that he would not come back. It was only much later that I found out how he died. Towards the end of the war, the Arrow Cross guards forced the remaining men of his unit into a hut which they soaked with petrol and burned to the ground.

People returning home from hiding or the camps had fantastic stories to tell, but I was not much interested in the tales of bravery and coincidences to which they owed their lives. Others must have felt the same about me. I noticed how my sister had to brace herself to listen to my talk about the camp. There was a popular cartoon which showed a man tied to a chair, with his friend facing him. The caption read:

'Now, if you like, I'll tell you how I survived the war.'

I did not seek out those fellow inmates I knew who had also returned. Unlike army veterans, survivors of concentration camps had no wish to get together to exchange their memories. Those who really wanted to know were the relatives of the dead, like the mother of sixteen year old Marika, a Young Zionist I had met in the forest camp in Poland. She was one of the unfortunates who had been unaware of her pregnancy until almost the last moment. In late Autumn, she gave birth to a baby girl in the 'medical' hut. They said that she had lived long enough to see the baby, who died shortly after her.

'My beautiful Marika!' sobbed her mother when she came to see me. 'Please tell me about her. How did she die? Somebody told my sister that she died in childbirth. Why do people invent such horrible lies? I knew my daughter, she was still a child. Please set my mind to rest, please tell me the truth!'

I looked at her. 'Of course she didn't have a baby,' I said, 'I was there and I knew her well. Whoever told you that was lying.'

Her relief shone across the tears. 'Thank God!' she said, 'You're telling the truth, aren't you? Would you swear that you're telling the truth?'

'I'll swear on anything you want. Marika died because she didn't get enough food; she just faded away.'

In a sea of uncertainties, there was one thing I knew for sure: I wanted to go to university. But how does one go about it? Universities had been all but closed to Jewish students for a long time and I knew no-one of my generation who had studied there. Did one just walk into the building and ask to be registered? Or did you have to know someone who was familiar with the place and who would introduce you? Or what? Imre Székely's mother was distantly related to an old Professor of Mathematics and offered to take me to see him.

The Professor did not quite understand what we wanted of him, especially when I made it clear that I abhorred Mathematics. He patted me kindly on the arm and said that the new political regime had changed the universities. Part of the teaching staff had been sacked and the curriculum was under review. New subjects were being introduced and the Faculty of Arts would admit anyone who had been prevented from studying in the past. The results of my final exams at grammar school would not matter. The gates were wide open for everyone, he said, since those who could not make it would soon drop out.

An admirable system. The only remaining question was the subject to be studied. Aunt Helen wanted it to be Chemistry so that, in time, I should be able to take over Uncle Marci's shop, but I didn't want to hear of it. I would study Philosophy, which included Psychology and Sociology, neither of which had the status of independent disciplines at the time. If you wanted to study Psychology, you had to take Philosophy as the main subject. My interest in Psychology went back to the time when I had not even known that such a subject existed. It had begun at the age of eight or nine, when I made the dramatic discovery that adults were unable to understand what children felt and thought. It was on the morning on which my mother slapped my face for being cheeky that I worked it out. Something was done to people that made them forget what it was like to be a child. Perhaps they were given an injection, or there was a ritual which they had to undergo at the age of about nineteen, to black out everything they'd thought and felt before. I could not ask the grownups about it because I knew that they were united in keeping their adult secrets from children. Would this happen to me too? I decided to fight it. I might not be able to escape the injection or spell, or whatever it was they would do to me, but I could defeat it by keeping a record of every minute of my life. I would write down everything I thought and did, from the moment I woke up until I fell asleep at night. A document of childhood like this needed, of course, a secret code which I set about inventing at once, by substituting each letter of the alphabet with the next.

Alas! the scheme did not work since, the very next day, I found it almost impossible to read what I'd written, but the need to remember my childhood remained with me. I often returned to it in adolescence as I tried, in desperation, to understand why my daily resolutions came to nothing. Was I not master of my own behaviour? What made me say and do things which I should not have done? I had great hopes of Psychology.

Sociology was a different matter. It was the study of the works of Marx and Engels, and included everything that Lenin and Stalin had written. Just as well that I had to take it up as part of my package, because Marxism–Leninism was an obligatory subject in all departments from Metallurgy to Medicine.

The Faculty of Arts was situated in a splendid old building with an imposing facade from which steps led to the Ring Road. I descended and ascended those steps majestically several times to make it clear to people in the street that I was part of it. They did not have to know that, at the registration office, I had just been advised to take some seminars, and that I did not dare ask what seminars were, nor where I was supposed to take them.

The first year syllabus still adhered to the old 'Artes Liberales' system in which students were free to decide which lectures they wanted to attend. There was a list of lecture courses pinned to the wall from which one chose. Bookshops and libraries had been damaged or looted, so that books had to be supplemented by mimeographed handouts. It was all tremendously exciting. I was doggedly reading excerpts from Kant and Leibnitz, and followed the ebb and flow of the crowd from one lecture room to another. Somehow, the system worked, since I remember surviving several orals, even before the second year when teaching began in earnest.

One of the perks of being at university was the distribution of sweet condensed milk and corned beef by an American charity. It must have been connected to the Marshall plan, since it dried up when the government refused American aid. Such heavenly food could be exchanged for cash but I never had the strength to do so. I was permanently ravenous.

'I don't know what to do,' I wailed to my sister, 'in less than a year, I've almost doubled my weight. I look monstrous. It makes me sick to catch my horrible reflection in a shop window.'

'Nonsense, stop exaggerating,' she said, 'of course you'd put on weight after the concentration camp. Everybody does. To call yourself monstrous and horrible is just childish.'

But she had to admit I had a problem. For nearly a year after my return I was suffering from a phantom hunger which couldn't be alleviated until I reached the point of vomiting. I would raid my sister's pantry for yesterday's leftovers and get up in the middle of the night to find something to eat. Many survivors had the same problem. Their conspicuous bulk triggered derisive comments. 'They must have fed these Jews well!' people sniggered when they saw them. I could not stop eating until, during a session on my analyst's couch, I understood that my pathological hunger had earlier roots than starvation in the camps. The insight resulted in a spectacular loss of weight. My normal eating habits returned although the spectre of obesity has haunted me all my life.

One would think that my preoccupation with my weight would have been cured in Auschwitz. Many illnesses were. People suffering from dyspepsia, skin conditions, diabetes, or goitre, ceased to be ill and were able to concentrate on the daily business of survival. The same happened to mental pain. Depression, insomnia, obsessions and anxiety states, aspects of the self which one would like to cut out like a sick growth, suddenly ceased to exist. Extreme deprivation is a universal panacea. The startling thing was that pain and misery came rushing back as soon as the circumstances became normal. I think that the suicide of survivors like Primo Levi was not simply a direct consequence of the camps. It was the realisation that escape from death was possible but escape from oneself was not.

What did I live on during the university years? The answer must have been *treacle* like the three sisters in *Alice in Wonderland* who lived in a well. My room in Aunt Helen's former flat was free, so was the analysis, and I must have accepted my meals as casually from Aunt Helen as I had done as a child. For as long as houses could still be privately owned, I received rent from my father's house in St Lőrinc. For a short time, I had a part-time job looking after a little girl with Down's syndrome. What else? I don't remember having been seriously affected by lack of money. I could not buy much anyway, since the shops had very little to sell. Unless you discovered that your second cousin went to the same school as the brother-in-law of the shop assistant's fiancé, it was unlikely that she would bring out the last pair of leather shoes from under the counter.

It was about the time of my return to Budapest that inflation spiralled out of all reason. The price of a loaf of bread rose from six pengoes to sixty, then to six hundred, sixty thousand, six million... The food queues snaked along streets and around blocks of buildings. The country, brought to its knees by defeat, accepted its misery.

No audible protest was heard against the occupying Russian forces either. The Germans had defended Budapest against the incoming tide of the Red Army for an unreasonably long time, even though, by then, Germany had all but lost the war. When the exhausted Russians finally took the city, many went on the rampage. They looted, and raped every female from young teenagers to old women. According to eyewitnesses they had behaved as if they had encountered a totally alien culture. They were fascinated by wristwatches. Girls I knew told me how they were gang-raped by soldiers sporting dozens of wristwatches on their arms. Their officers organised frequent raids on ordinary pedestrians who were then taken away at gunpoint, to replenish the workforce in Minsk or Outer Mongolia. Officially, of course, the rape and looting never happened. The Russians were our liberators, and Stalin, the wise and benevolent father of nations, smiled at us from pictures and posters everywhere.

I told myself that the first wave of the Red Army that entered Budapest probably came from some dark corner of Asia where victors were expected to behave like this. The Russians I'd met in Poland had been different. The Red Army had, after all, saved Europe from the Nazis and I owed my life to them. So did many of the surviving Jews who were flocking into the newly established Communist Party. A small nucleus of old Communists, who had been cruelly persecuted by the previous regime, had taken over key positions, but other political parties were still in existence. I was canvassing enthusiastically for the forthcoming election, which, had I but known it, would be the last one worthy of the name. I applied to become a Party member and was put on three month probation.

The admission procedure was a public affair in a large hall in the presence of the communist members of the staff and students of the Faculty. The panel sat behind a table, elevated on a dais, with the candidate standing on the floor in front of them. The Party Secretary was consulting my file.

'How do you propose to fight the enemy within?'

'Have you ever been a churchgoer?' It felt like a mixture of a police interrogation and a confessional. It soon came to light that my father had owned a shop in which he had employed a shop assistant. As a daughter of a capitalist, I was rejected.

From a persecuted Jew, I had now become a bourgeois, the consequences of which I was soon to realise. At that moment, I was merely sorry for not being allowed to join a club which seemed to me the most desirable of all.

2

Józsi was only two years older, but an adult compared to me. Calmly accepting my chaotic time-keeping, he would wait for me in front of the University building for a long time, and would merely shake his head when I arrived. He kept safety pins in his pocket, knowing that the fastenings for my skirt or girdle had a tendency to give up the ghost, and once he even presented me with a kirby grip.

'Wouldn't it be easier to sew a button on your cardigan?' he asked with resignation as we were sitting on the steps under the arcade of the House of Parliament. Here, or the park, were the only places where we could have privacy. Józsi lived with his parents in a small flat, and I, the proud owner of an independent room in the Hajós Street flat, was never safe from Aunt Helen popping in for this and that, even when Józsi was there. Privacy for my generation was a rare asset which became even more precious when we were in love. There were no digs to rent and hotels demanded one's identity card for registering with the police. The woods of the Buda hills offered their fragrant depths readily enough in the summer, but no desire was so intense that it could brave a Hungarian winter out-of-doors. To make love in a car did not enter the realms of our imagination, any more than the possibility of owning one.

I had known Józsi as a Zionist, a movement he had scornfully discarded in favour of Communism. We both felt that the Jewish question was one part only of the world's problems. I was immersed in Karl Marx but Józsi was not one for theories.

When the opportunity arrived to go to University, he chose instead to become a radio mechanic.

As a result, he was rolling in money. He had no workshop, but made house calls, to which I sometimes accompanied him. He would carefully detach the radio from the socket in the wall, unscrew its back panel and examine it with the concentration of a surgeon, about to operate. Impressed by the multi-coloured tangle of wires, the owner would timidly ask him if the radio could be repaired. Józsi would be cautiously optimistic, without revealing that the severity of the radio's condition largely depended on how much time he was prepared to spend on it. In acute cases of financial shortage, he fiddled for hours with a set which he could have mended in minutes.

He was of medium height, slim, a little short-sighted, and became my boy-friend almost without my noticing it. He quietly ousted Eli Bohrer and simply annexed me. I liked his slow drawl, which remained the same whether he was talking to a baby or a Party boss. He was a committed member of the Communist Party but had little to say during the heated discussions, which could have lifted an air balloon. I liked his calmness, his practical sense, and that he always knew exactly what he wanted.

Just then he wanted to go to bed with me. 'You're twenty-three, for God's sake,' he argued, 'Do you want to die a virgin?'

I took a deep breath and told him that Aunt Helen was going away for two days. No announcement in history has been greeted with greater enthusiasm than this. 'Wednesday, then,' he said after the last kiss in the doorway, 'Wednesday at three o'clock.'

But it was not so simple. Tossing and turning on the analyst's couch, I realised the dilemma facing me. The sofa bed in my room was adequate for kissing and cuddling, but was I expected to make up the bed when it came to the Real Thing? It seemed a wanton thing to do. I opened the sofa bed as a rehearsal and put on the sheet, then removed the sheet and closed the bed. It looked uninviting. I opened it again and, oh yes, a friend had said that I would need a towel on top of the sheet. What for? I can't do this. Only a prostitute would receive a man with her bed all made up. Why can't I just run away? When the bed was finally made up at three o'clock, Józsi wasn't there.

Half past three, four o'clock and Józsi still had not arrived. He came nearly two hours later, having run all the way. He did not invent an excuse but said that, just before leaving home, he'd fallen asleep in his father's armchair.

I was puzzled. Then it began to dawn on me that men, too, have their anxieties.

I had known Lili only by sight, until I noticed her sitting on the grass in the middle of a courtyard in the university, as far from other students as space allowed. Somehow, I took her isolation as a challenge, and went to speak to her. She was surprised but pleased, and we left together for the next lecture. It was the beginning of a friendship of more than half a century. Fifty years of loyalty and betrayal, fierce competition and mutual support, and I still stay with her and her sister Magda when I visit Budapest. But, as to the beginning of our friendship, Lili disagrees with me. She insists that there was no courtyard; that she was not sitting alone; and does not remember that I took the initiative.

'But you remember when you bought the condom?' I asked.

'Of course, I remember, but that was much later. By then we'd been friends for quite a while,' she said.

We had been planning a party in celebration of our tutor's victory over an MP who wanted to remove Darwin's theory of evolution from the schoolbooks. I had written a parody of the debate which needed to be illustrated by several objects including – I don't remember why – a condom. How could we get hold of one? A man could ask for it in a whisper at the chemist shop, making sure that no female was present, but for a girl it was unthinkable to do the same. I chickened out of the idea, but Lili tossed her head and declared that she was going to buy one. She put on her coat and departed, leaving me speechless with admiration. History knew many brave women, but I doubted if any of them would have walked into a shop and boldly ask for a condom.

'I've never been so impressed in my life as when you returned with the box,' I told her many years later.

'I should hope so,' she giggled, 'but I think it's time to tell you that I didn't do it. I was standing in front of the chemist shop and couldn't bring myself to enter when I spotted the brother of a school-friend on the other side of the road. He doubled up with laughter when I told him what wanted, but he went into the shop and bought a packet.'

Lili was studying the same subjects as me. She had no room of her own in her parents' flat, so we revised at my place.

Political Economy demanded a level of abstract thinking for which the grammar school had not prepared us. Eventually, however, the fog began to lift and we shouted with delight when we understood a difficult passage. I had begun to understand the complex arguments and elegant refutations of *Das Kapital* and my delight in them had no limits. Marx had introduced me to the world of abstract ideas and, for that, I am eternally grateful to him. What it did not teach me was to question what I read. At the age of twenty, my mind was yearning for certainty. I had found it in Dialectical Materialism.

'Listen to this,' I said to Lili, who was sitting on the floor with her notes scattered around her, "The maximum rate of profit is only settled by the continuous struggle between capital and labour. The capitalist constantly tends to reduce wages while extending the working day, while the working man constantly presses in the opposite direction." It explains everything. I wonder if anyone has ever tried to dispute it.'

'They must have tried it in England or America,' Lili assumed, 'unless Marx is on their blacklist of publications.'

'He must be,' I agreed, 'otherwise they would have had a revolution. No wonder that people have been sent to prison for just having a copy.'

One had only to look around to see how right the Comrades were. The peasants lived in abject poverty because land was owned by a few families who had more in common with their aristocratic relatives in Europe than with their tenants. Factory owners built expensive villas in Buda while the workers lived in slums. 'They will never give up what they have peacefully,' Józsi said, 'until we come to power.' He was ready to fight the forces of Evil but the fighting had already been done by the Red Army which had liberated us. Thanks to them the transfer of private property to the state would be bloodless.

Józsi, who had set his heart on marrying me, achieved the impossible: he got a flat. Money could not have done it, but Józsi had connections within the Party. He took me to see it and talked about a wedding in a registry office. I wasn't sure about the wedding, but the flat delighted me.

Freedom Hill (as it became called) was an area of outstanding scenic beauty at the top end of the cogwheel tram-track in Buda. Some entrepreneurs had built a few luxury flats there before the war. They were meant for the rich with a car to get there. We took a tram to Buda, changed to the cogwheel tram, and then walked. The flat consisted of one room with a bathroom and kitchenette. It had a balcony and the window opened onto a panorama. Over the treetops of Buda one could see the twisting blue ribbon of the Danube behind which Pest shimmered in the distance, like a fairy-tale city. Behind the house was a meadow with wild flowers and buzzing, humming, insects, which knew nothing of pesticides. The curly white clouds, grazing in the sky, knew nothing of aerial bombing either.

The following week, we moved into the flat. By good luck, my sister was moving house and had bought new furniture, so that we got their sofa bed, two armchairs, and a glass-fronted wardrobe. I had, of course, no idea that my new life with Józsi would only last for just over a year. Since the Party was surprisingly moralistic about people living together without the blessing of the state, Józsi was pressing for marriage, but I found more excuses than Penelope warding off her suitors. Józsi, however, was in a strong position, because I had nowhere else to go. The housing shortage made renting impossible, and the room in Hajós Street had long gone. But marriage was for life, and I couldn't imagine myself living with Józsi for that long.

Józsi was magnanimous. When we finally parted, it was he who left, taking only the superb radio which was the envy of our friends. The flat became mine. Józsi, who never understood that I was not in love with him, rang me at regular intervals, asking if I'd changed my mind, but gave up, in the end. We had lost touch for years before he became a high ranking officer in the dreaded Secret Police.

I must tell you about the sale of my father's house. It began with official letters demanding that I pay the rates, and the bills for water and sewerage, and other such nonsense. I was not interested. After my return from the concentration camp, I had no wish to see my father's house, or to go to St Lőrinc. The envelopes became irritating and vaguely threatening, so I put them, unopened, into a drawer. It took two years for a second drawer to overflow. I did not know what to do about it until much later when I was already working as a labourer and, to my consternation, my pay packet was stopped. The solicitor to whom I presented a suitcase full of unopened letters was not very nice to me, but managed to sell the house and pay off my debts. The blue dressing gown and the leather briefcase, on which I spent the remains of the money, became legendary with my friends, and remembered by them for years.

3

Almost all the Psychology that I'd learned in the late 1940s is obsolete today. Out of the twelve human instincts postulated by McDougall, I only remember the instincts of self-assertion, and the instinct of love of parents. There was Watson's Behaviourism and Köhler's Gestalt psychology – and I wasn't even aware that they contradicted each other. In the long run, however, it did not matter. My real education took place in M.'s seminars at Maria Terézia Square. Maria Terézia, the old empress of the Austro-Hungarian Monarchy, seemed to haunt me. The grammar school where I'd learnt nearly nothing, and the Institute where M. introduced us to scientific research, were both named after her.

M. was a scholar and a politician, but most of all a teacher. It is impossible to exaggerate the impact he had on us during those Saturday morning seminars. Everyone suspected that Eva S. had agreed to emigrate to Brazil with her parents only in order to avoid presenting an ill-prepared essay for M. She returned thirty years later – and confessed the truth of this.

His influence on my thinking was for life. Every time when, during a discussion, I try to concentrate on the matter in hand rather than winning the argument, or check out a fact rather than letting it dangle unresolved in the air, or persist in reading a difficult text for no other reason than to fight my innate laziness, it is to emulate him. It was from him that I learned how to make good coffee by letting the steam percolate slowly across freshly ground beans, that prints or posters on the wall were preferable to cheap reproductions, that it was more attractive to walk gracefully in flat shoes than wobble on high heels, that nothing should be called beautiful merely by virtue of being ornate.

'I have lived through all the great adventures and experiences my century offered,' M. said many decades later, during an interview. He was talking about his youth in Paris and the years at the Sorbonne when war broke out and he returned to Budapest. He survived the labour camp and had a meteoric career, followed by a long imprisonment because of his part in the

'56 Uprising. The journalist who interviewed him towards the end of his life wisely kept quiet about the Leporello list of his conquests among women, which would have been almost as long as the index of his publications. What gave us young women the idea that men do not have to be good looking? My friends and I would have turned our backs on the Apollo of Belvedere on grounds that there were insufficient brains in his marble head. M. was unassuming in appearance, a slender bespectacled Jew in a shabby suit. Yet all his students were, to some degree, in love with him. People with great charisma are always surrounded by disciples whose partial loss of sanity is similar to being in love.

The condition for my admittance to the Saturday seminar was to give a thirty minute presentation summarising Wilhelm Köhler's book, *The Mentality of Apes*. Köhler, one of the Berlin 'Gestalt' psychologists who were involved in studying intelligence, had gone to Tenerife in 1913 to work with apes, in order to outline the upper limit of their mental abilities. The hero of his book was a chimpanzee called Sultan, who was able to solve many of the ingenious puzzles which Köhler and his research team tried out on him. Köhler was impressed by the animal's facial expression of 'I've got it!' when he suddenly grasped a solution, and called it the 'Aha' experience. I knew how Sultan felt. The 'Aha' experience is the link between Archimedes and the child who manages to tie his shoelaces for the first time.

I had worked so hard for the presentation at Maria Terézia Square that I still remember the two experiments which I used to summarise the book. In both of them, a group of chimpanzees, including Sultan, found themselves in a large cage with bananas hanging loosely – but out of reach – from a net on the ceiling. In the first experiment, hollow sticks were thrown into the cage. The sticks were too short to reach the net but one stick inserted into another would have done the trick. 'Unlike humans, apes are unable to create or use tools,' I concluded. In the other experiment, there were no sticks. The chimpanzees could only reach the bananas if one of them could stand still for long enough for another to stand on his shoulders. 'Unlike humans, chimpanzees are unable to co-operate to achieve a goal,' I said.

All wrong? Of course it was all wrong. You should have been at the grammar school a few years previously when I got a first because I correctly answered the question whether man would ever land on the moon. I proved that it would be impossible, using gravity and the stratosphere as my arguments. Portable telephones? Aircraft faster than sound? Science fiction was not part of the curriculum.

I was in my third year at the University, with one more to go, when M. became head of the Institute of Education, which designed the curriculum for the country's primary schools. Although I had, as yet, no degree, he gave me a job there. I had a desk but, for the life of me, I cannot remember what I was to do. My main activity, I think, was to write a thesis on young children's understanding of Geography. Shortly after I submitted it, a furious M. summoned me to his office. It turned out that I had submitted a draft of my thesis without inserting the page numbers, and full of pencilled corrections. The examiner, knowing that I was M.'s pupil, telephoned him asking what she should do with it. The thesis could not have been too bad, since after all, I got my degree.

4

1948 was a year of digging and scaffolding, of people hanging onto trams like bunches of grapes. It was a year of beans and lentils and boarded-up shops. It was a year when seamstresses could transform men's shirts into blouses, blankets into overcoats. The presence of the Soviet Army was evident everywhere. In March, the snow became an ugly grey slush, and the road was full of potholes. It was into this drab and depressing existence that the news of a foreign grant burst like a meteor.

UNICEF, the child-centred branch of the United Nations, had invited professional people from Eastern Europe to attend a course in Paris on child-related studies. The distribution of places followed the mysterious route of all foreign scholarships. Neither Lili nor I had published anything, so how did we get selected? The miracle could not have been more stunning had the grant come literally out of the blue, drifting through the air into M.'s hand.

'There is no question of you deserving it,' he had said, when he told me that I had got a place, 'You show talent, although for my life I can't discover what you're talented in. What you need, I suppose, is to grow up, and there's no better place for that than Paris.' He loaded Lili and me with extra work to make sure that we spent time in the *Bibliotheque Nationale*.

The dress I had made for Paris was white, with small blue flowers, and, in it, I felt like dancing on air. Józsi went pale when he saw me, but manfully helped with the complicated business of getting a travel permit. He made me promise to write regularly, and borrowed a presentable suitcase for me. I can still see him waving goodbye on the platform of the Western Terminal, the same platform on which Aunt Helen stood forlornly ten years later when I left Hungary.

Study Leave - a story.

It was a blue and gold April day when Lili and I arrived in Paris. The train journey from Budapest (after a change in Prague) took thirty-six hours. The sleeping car was wood-panelled and carpeted and had a curtain on the door which could be pulled down for privacy, and a washbasin with a special shelf for a tooth mug. In the evening, the attendant came in and made up the beds with fresh linen and placed woollen blankets on a shelf in case we should need them later.

'Pinch me,' Lili said, 'Is this real? I thought that such splendour had disappeared with the monarchy.'

'It's fantastic,' I agreed.

'Do you remember the time when people used to go abroad for their holidays?' she asked, stretching herself luxuriously on the bed. 'I went to Abbazia with my parents before the war. What about you?'

'Aunt Helen used to send me to holiday camps in Austria. The last time I went abroad I was eleven. Unless we count Auschwitz as going abroad,' I added.

Lili yawned. 'I don't think you can. Shall we switch off the light?'

'I will, but let's not forget that when we arrive we must talk to somebody about accommodation. I'd rather share a room with you than with a stranger.'

But the representative waiting for us at the terminal was busy with porters and taxis and didn't understand what we were trying to tell him. We were driven to an elegant hotel near the Parthenon where somebody took me up to my room. Did I say room? It was a suite with a private bathroom and balcony and an internal telephone. Lili had a similar one on the same floor. I quickly rang her and asked her to ring back. It worked. From then on we would phone each other as soon as we parted in the corridor.

Armed with notebooks and a dictionary we departed every morning for the Sorbonne to listen to a lecture we only partly understood, then we went to the splendid Bibliotheque Nationale where I had to make notes on 'The Wild Boy of Aveyron', an assignment given by M. The UNICEF organisers used the course as benevolent propaganda with which to dazzle professionals from Eastern Europe. The group, in which Lili and I were the only students, consisted of paediatricians, educationalists and architects, for whom this was the last chance to see what Western democracies did for their children. We visited schools, nurseries, children's hospitals in Holland and Belgium, and made a short visit to London. We were treated as VIP's, and the grant they gave us was more than generous.

It was shortly after our arrival that I rang Lili to remind her of the dance at the Cité Universitaire. She said she was busy. I put down the receiver and went to investigate. I found her on top of her bed, spreading hot wax on her legs. The label on the jar informed us that its contents were a breakthrough in science which solved the problem of unwanted hair. The rest of the wax was bubbling in a heating apparatus on the table and smelt like a cauldron of hot tar.

The problem being specific to Lili, I grinned and pointed out that in the Middle Ages people used to pour the stuff down from the ramparts of besieged castles, although the enemy must have died from the smell alone. I advised her to come to the dance instead, but she said it was too late because the wax had begun to dry on her legs.

In the end, I had to go on my own. The dance was a noisy and colourful affair, mostly attended by foreign students. A few unattached young men were standing around, but they took no notice of me. I was wondering whether to admit defeat and go back to the hotel when a dark haired young man materialised at my elbow.

'Do you know anybody in this crowd?' he asked.

He said that he despised dances but now that we were both here we might as well join the others. I agreed. He said that he was studying architecture and asked where I came from. I told him that it was Hungary and he said that he would honestly never have guessed it, but, of course, there was nothing wrong with that. He said that he was Turkish, and I said that we had defeated the Turks in 1686. Then we danced again, and he asked if I liked Paris. I said that I did, but that now I was going back to the hotel. He said that he would take me home.

It was one of those occasions when the inability to find my way was nearly my downfall. We walked for a long time before I realised I was nowhere near my hotel.

'But I don't live here,' I protested, when we arrived.

'Don't worry,' he answered, 'I do. Come up to my room and I'll make you a cup of Turkish coffee.'

'I certainly won't. I thought we were going to my hotel.'

The young man from Turkey threw up his arms in desperation. 'How provincial can you get? We are not on the Great Hungarian Plains for God's sake. Stop behaving as if I wanted to seduce you! Don't you realise we're in Paris? It's customary for a girl to visit the man with whom she's been dancing all evening.'

'Is it? I didn't know,' I said humbly. He assured me that it was.

'We have to sit on the bed,' he said when we arrived to his room on the fifth floor. There was only one chair stacked with books.

'Let me unbutton your blouse. It's quite in order,' he added when I protested, 'In Paris you do as the Parisians do.'

He was quite cross when I pushed him away and told him in French mixed with Hungarian what I thought of him. He had the decency, however, to take me back to my hotel where I went straight to Lili's room to report.

Lili didn't protest when I switched on the light. She sat up in the bed and blinked at me.

'Turkish?' she said in horror. 'Have you taken leave of you senses? Didn't you know that all Turks have venereal disease?'

'Have they? I didn't know,' I said humbly, for the second time that evening. The vision of a very sick nation couldn't get hold of my imagination, however, since Lili, at this point, got out of bed and began to limp towards the bathroom.

'What happened to your legs?' I cried.

'The wax wouldn't come off when it got dry,' she said tersely, 'Never mind my legs. Józsi telephoned from Budapest and you were not here. He sounded really upset. Have you written to him?'

I was taken aback. The thought of Józsi hadn't crossed my mind all evening. I had written to him a week ago. I had even put the letter in an envelope. Moreover, I had gone to the Tabac next door specially to buy a stamp. I clearly remembered the feeling, as I put the envelope inside my dictionary, of a job well done.

'Have you seen my French-Hungarian dictionary,' I asked Lili, 'I've left it somewhere. I hoped that it was in your room.'

How can I tell you what Paris was like? I see myself holding on to the pivot on a merry-go-round, with my eyes half closed against the burst of radiance around me. Oh, for the smell and sound of Paris, the musty bookshops and white and gold restaurants, the fish markets and the excursions to Versailles! Oh, for the golden boys chatting you up, insisting that you'd met before in Marseilles or Annecy or perhaps 'sur un bateau...?' Don't ask me what I learned from the lectures, what I saw on the visits to Amsterdam or London. In Brussels, they gave us a reception in the Hotel de Ville. I remember the tapestries, and that the hors d'oeuvres was served on real shells. In Antwerp, there was a play group to which only fair-haired children seemed to be admitted. In London, they took us to a medieval hall where toys made by fathers for their children were exhibited, nobody understood why. In Oxford, it was raining, which was just as well because the unreality of it made me quite dizzy.

In the meantime, I was falling in love with a Bulgarian architect, but I gave him up for a fair haired Czech, only to find that he had fallen for somebody else. I liked the Bulgarian, but I was also a little in love with Lili's handsome Italian and retrospectively in love with M. who'd sent us to Paris. All this had nothing to do with Józsi, who lived on a different planet.

I didn't like to think about going home. The end of the course was approaching with the speed of an express train. Lili and I wrote urgent letters to M. begging him to let us stay longer. Our arguments for extra time involved libraries, and important research units which, as somebody later told us, made him laugh out loud when he read our letter. To our great surprise, however, he agreed for us to stay another month after the course.

Towards the end, I began furiously to save up so that I had a little money left. It did not matter that we had to leave the hotel or that the grand dinners at the Cité Universitaire had come to an end. We were happy to live the life of penniless students. Paris was generous to the young, and allowed us, for a while, to believe we were her legitimate children.

But even an extended stay comes to an end. The second class tickets for which we had exchanged our first class ones had a date on them. We shook hands with our friends, who said that they hoped to see us in Paris once more – which had about as much reality as a rendezvous on the moon. The news from home was not encouraging. Two people from the Hungarian delegation had asked for asylum. The possibility of not returning fleetingly crossed our minds, but Lili had elderly parents at home whom she could not abandon, and I could not imagine living away from my sister.

We were utterly dejected on the day of departure. Lili was making sandwiches for the journey very slowly, as if she was hoping for a miracle before we got on the train.

'Look at the clock!' I cried, 'Are you packed?'

'More or less,' Lili said, slicing the bread.

'For God's sake stop that and finish your packing!'

'I have to do this or we'll have nothing to eat on the train. This one won't be a first class sleeper, with breakfast in the restaurant car.'

'We won't get on the train at all unless you hurry up. I'll go and get a taxi.'

There were no taxis to be seen. I ran to the main road, but all the cruising taxis were occupied. The dingy little hotel to which we'd moved after the course had no telephone. Blast Lili! I'd relied on her. To make things worse, it started to rain. I became more cross and wet with every minute, so that when a taxi came I found myself shouting.

'Can you take me to the station? Quickly please or we'll miss the train! No, not that way. We must go to the hotel first to pick up my friend and the luggage.'

The driver made a face but I didn't want to see it. 'It is only four suitcases. Only hurry, please, because we'll be late!' I urged him, as I jumped in the taxi. He swerved and stopped in front of the hotel. Lili was nowhere to be seen.

'Could you come up with me? It is only the fourth floor. Please!' I felt awful, because I knew that he wouldn't be satisfied with the tip. We had little cash left after booking-out of the hotel, enough only for the fare. It couldn't be helped; this was an emergency. Luckily, he appreciated it, and helped to carry the luggage. He piled the suitcases into the car, slammed the door and put his foot on the accelerator. The big clock at the Terminal reassured us that we were in good time.

'Bon voyage,' the driver said, as he helped us unload the car, 'I'm glad you've made it!'

'You've been very helpful,' I said gratefully. Lili was fishing money from her purse, 'How much?' she asked.

The driver looked surprised. 'But I'm not a taxi!' he protested, 'I stopped because you waved and shouted that unless I took you to the station you'd miss the train.'

5

Józsi – from whom I had not yet separated – was waiting for me as I stepped off the Paris express. I looked around in a daze. Had Budapest always been so small? The houses seemed to have shrunk, and I noticed how badly broken the pavements were, with potholes and puddles everywhere.

Józsi was angry. 'You arrive home and the only thing you see is the potholes. What we have achieved is nothing to you, only what is still amiss. And don't think that going abroad was such a good thing. You'll have to do a lot of convincing that it didn't have a bad influence on you.'

'Józsi, listen, I've seen the sea! The coach driver heard that Lili and I had never seen it, and he made a detour on his way to Brussels. He stopped behind some sand dunes. Are you listening? We got out of the coach and ran across the dunes and there it was. It is without end, and it's really salty. I tasted it.'

Józsi heaved my luggage onto a tram and said that a second telephone had been installed in the house, so that the tenants did not have to go down to the ground floor every time it rang. We missed the cogwheel tram and had to wait, Józsi with impatient anticipation. 'I've bought new things for the flat,' he said 'Just wait until you see it.'

'I must tell you this,' I said, 'When the coach arrived at Amsterdam, late in the evening, there were students waiting to take us to the houses of university staff who offered to put us up for the night. I tried to tell the boy that I had no Dutch money to pay the concierge but he didn't understand me. All the houses had gardens in front – they live quite differently there – and you can imagine how embarrassed I was when he rang the bell and a man in shirtsleeves came out. I apologised for not having any change but he didn't understand me either. We went straight into a dining room where he introduced me to his family.'

'I bet they had servants,' Józsi said, 'It's easy to impress you.'

'No, but listen. Somebody took me upstairs to a room with a bed and I fell asleep at once. Next morning I was woken by another man in a striped vest – you may be right, I think he was a servant – who brought me a cup of tea and a small piece of biscuit on a tray. Imagine! A cup of tea and nothing else for breakfast. I was ravenous.'

'Here is the tram,' Józsi said,' Mind your handbag, I'll take the suitcase.'

I couldn't finish my story which had the happy ending of my host catching me just before I left. A Dutch breakfast of coffee and pâté and ham and cold meat and cheeses was something to be remembered in the lean years to come.

1948 was the year when the Communist Party assumed total power. Passports were withdrawn, letters were censored, and international telephone calls were stopped. Stalin's fatherly face beamed down from posters in every office, schoolroom and public place. I watched in horrified disbelief as his benign smile changed into a sadistic grin, but Józsi, who had his feet on the ladder of the Party hierarchy, did not see it.

Paris became a legend. In less than a year – a year in which the political climate became worse – it receded into the distant past like some sunlit Arcadia never to be seen again. It was a year later that Lili discovered someone who had a friend who had been granted a trip to France as member of a commercial delegation. She entered into negotiations and got hold of a packet of 'Caporal Bleu' cigarettes. It was such a treasure that she threw a party on the strength of it, offering a cigarette to each of us. I shut my eyes and inhaled deeply. The smell reminded me of petrol fumes in the Rue Vaugirard and the air in the Metro on a rainy day. Paradise was lost for ever and I felt like crying.

True Democracy - a story.

The person I least expected to see again was Dr Wang from the study group in Paris. He was a serious and polite Chinese who had kept himself apart from the kaleidoscope of the rapidly changing groupings within the course. Impeccably dressed in a dark three piece suit, even in summer, he attended every lecture without fail but said little about himself. The only thing we knew about him was that he came from Hong Kong and intended to settle in Paris after the course. And now, to my utter surprise, he wrote to a colleague to say that he was coming to attend a medical conference in Budapest, and would be pleased to meet his friends from the course.

I rang Lili, who was also thrilled. 'Fancy seeing him again,' she said, 'Dr. Wang of all people. How did he get his visa?'

Józsi asked the same question. 'There's something fishy about this,' he said, 'Somebody must have arranged it for him. What does a Chinese doctor want in Hungary?'

'He wrote to Dr. Barna who is head of the children's wing in the hospital. They met in Paris.'

'Exactly,' Józsi said, 'What do you think an imperialist organisation like the UNICEF gave Dr. Barna a grant for? They've probably recruited him as a subversive. You should never have gone on that course.'

I had no intention of entering into the familiar quarrel which was beginning to sound like a scratch on an old record.

'He must be all right if he's got an entry visa,' I said, 'Do you think that the Ministry of Internal Affairs is less vigilant than you?'

Józsi didn't want to argue either. 'I tell you what. If he is really interested in seeing the country we could drive him around to show things.'

My heart sank, 'I could certainly ask him.'

'He'll want to see the Balaton. It is, after all, the biggest lake in Europe. On the way we could visit the new power plant and we could take him to see the Pioneer Railway. The car should be all right now that I've mended the brakes.'

József's car caused a sensation among our friends. Nobody else I knew had a car. Cars had simply disappeared, together with the class that owned them. Józsi had an ancient DKW with a detachable hood and a perfectly sound hooter. It did not start easily, but its body was scientifically streamlined to counter air resistance. Air must have been more resilient when he drove uphill because it was then that the passengers were asked to push. Even though the road to Lake Balaton was fairly flat, Dr. Wang had no idea what he was agreeing to when we met in front of his hotel.

The Pioneer Railway was a short track through the Buda hills run by children under fourteen years of age. The guards and ticket collectors were members of the Pioneers, the Party's youth organization, and the railway was a showpiece to demonstrate what the People's Democracy could do for the young. Visiting Soviet dignitaries would have recognised it as a replica of their own, but Dr. Wang seemed somewhat puzzled as to why we went there.

Our visit caused a sensation, although not in the way Józsi had expected. The first Pioneer who saluted us ran to inform the others that there was a real Chinese man at the terminal, and in a minute we were surrounded. None of them had seen a Chinese person before, except in films, and everyone wanted to touch him. They asked him to put his signature in the visitors' book and to pose for a photograph. Some of the adult passengers deliberately missed the next train to walk up the platform to glance at him. A twelve year old ticket collector asked him to say something in Chinese. By the time we got away there was no time to visit the power plant and we drove straight to the lake.

To my relief the car started at once. 'I hope you don't mind if I drive without stopping,' Józsi remarked casually, 'we should be there in two hours and find a restaurant by the lake.'

It was a very hot day. The sun fused with a metallic blue-white sky which was painful to look at. To sit in an open car was a blessing but it gave no protection against the dust on the road. We passed through villages where drinks could have been had, but would the car start again? Józsi drove on. I turned back in my seat to keep up a desultory conversation in French, hoping that Dr. Wang was not very thirsty.

At last we arrived at Lelle, a popular resort on the lake. Józsi patted the rear of the DKW which had stopped obediently in the High Street opposite a pub.

Dr. Wang got out of the car brushing the dust from his suit. I ran impatiently towards the pub garden but saw uniformed security guards flanking the gate. One of them barred my way.

'The pub is not open to the public,' he said, 'You can't go in.'

'Can we get in through the main door?'

'Are you deaf? I said that it wasn't open.'

Józsi tried the Party angle. 'We are parched, Comrade Officer. We have come all the way from Budapest without stopping and we badly need a drink. Could we get one for you as well?'

'You won't get into a pub in Lelle, that's for sure. The whole government is here for the celebrations. Now move away, will you?'

Of course! We had both forgotten that it was the anniversary of the poet József Attila, whom the party had adopted as its own. It was ten years since he had thrown himself under a train in Lelle. His statue was to be unveiled by the Minister of Education, Dr. Ortutay. It had to be something special to bring half the Ministry down to the Balaton on such a scorching day.

I looked longingly into the pub garden, where a long trestle table covered with white linen was tantalizingly set out for a meal, and saw the Minister, whose face was familiar from posters and newspapers, walking towards us. He was surrounded by dignitaries. One of them was Comrade Tompe, the Party Secretary of the district, the other was the Chief of Police.

The gate, flanked by the two Security guards was open. Józsi suddenly got hold of Dr. Wang and stepped inside. 'Comrade Minister,' he drawled, 'allow me to introduce Dr. Wang who is attending a medical conference in Budapest.'

It happened so quickly that the guards stood as if paralysed. A Chinese man in Lelle was clearly too much for them. Józsi linked his other arm into mine and calmly introduced me as well. Dr. Ortutay stopped, perplexed, and cast a reproachful glance at his entourage. He was, however, too experienced to let it be known that he did not recall Dr. Wang.

'Welcome to Lelle!' he said and shook hand with each of us in turn. 'I'm glad you could come. Shall we go and have some lunch?'

Józsi's colossal cheek left me speechless. The Minister of Education in person! These were times when one could get prosecuted even for publicly telling a joke against the Party. We could have been accused of spying. I could have been chucked out of the University, or worse. Still, I had no choice but to follow them to the top of the U-shaped table where Ortutay offered us the seats opposite himself and Comrade Tompe (I've often wondered since whose seats they were). However, scared I was, the chilled wine was marvelous, and the waiters were already approaching with the first course.

Dr. Wang politely thanked the Minister, who turned to me for translation. On top of everything I'd also have to act as an interpreter! I drank some more wine and tried to concentrate on my French.

When a few days later I described the scene to M., he roared with laughter. 'Didn't you know that Ortutay is one of the best French linguists? He'd been the cultural attaché in Paris for years. And you translated for him!' Then he calmed down. 'Of course, he couldn't talk a foreign language in front of the Comrades. But to pretend that he needed you to understand what Wang was saying!'

Even though I was drinking more than was good for me, I saw that Dr. Wang did not understand what was going on. It took him some time to realise that the man with whom he was chatting amiably was the Minister of Education. In the meantime our plates were heaped with food straight from a culinary fairy tale. Dr. Wang assured us that he liked Hungarian food as much as he had expected. I looked at Józsi who was wolfing it down and said that we were glad to hear it.

My fright was giving way to the spirit of adventure. *'Après nous la deluge,'* I giggled when Comrade Tompe asked us if we'd like to join him for a sail on the lake. To hell with the consequences! I knew that I would not have another opportunity to sail in a yacht as long as I lived.

Some yacht it was too. Defying the laws of physics, it was twice as large inside as out. The cabin was all teak and gleaming brass and hand-made folk art. I was immensely impressed. How was I to know that, in less than a year, Comrade Tompe would be executed for treason? The show trials were just about to start.

I held tight to a swaying table in the cabin.

'I wish it would stop wobbling,' was the last thing Józsi heard me say. The wine, the food and the fresh air on the lake were too much for me. Dr. Wang would have to translate for himself.

It was late afternoon when Józsi managed to shake some sense into me. 'We've arrived,' he said. 'We are back in Lelle. You must say goodbye to Comrade Ortutay and thank Comrade Tompe for the sail.'

I must have done so, because the next thing I remember was my overwhelming relief when I climbed into the car, next to Józsi. The sun setting behind the fence cast shadows like iron bars on the dusty road. Dr. Wang took his seat in the back.

'A most interesting experience,' he said, 'Do I take it that neither of you had met the Minister before?'

'We hadn't,' I said, 'but of course everybody knows his face from the papers.'

'Amazing!' said Dr. Wang, 'Yet he invited you for lunch and took you sailing. Your system of government is new to me but I can't deny that it is democratic. Truly democratic!'

He leaned back on the seat and braced himself for the return journey.

6

To work at the Institute of Education was a good thing, even if we hardly saw M. himself who moved in the rarefied circles of decision-making and political machinations. Still, those of us who had attended his seminars at Maria Terézia Square were regarded as belonging to his inner circle. I can still see Lili's bemused face when, after a lecture, M. had to leave before the enthusiastic clapping was over, and the audience only had us, his students, to congratulate on his brilliance. Lili and I accepted the handshakes without batting an eyelid, before collapsing in giggles.

The axe fell on us in 1951, on a Monday morning. I took an early cogwheel tram to be in the office for the obligatory half-hour discussion on the *Free People*, the Communist Party's daily newspaper. Everybody in the tram was busy scrutinising the statistics of a successful agricultural commune, knowing that the Party Secretary kept a record on their commitment to the People's Democracy. Passive acceptance of the regime was not enough. Those who were not members of the Party had even more reason to demonstrate their loyalty to the class struggle and to speak up at the meetings.

The *Free People* never reported ordinary crimes or the difficulties of everyday life. It informed its readers about the regional successes of the Three Year Plan and denounced the enemies of the people who sabotaged the distribution of consumer goods. Those responsible for the shortage of meat and bread were usually in an executive position. They were tried and imprisoned, but their punishment seldom brought any change.

The latest articles, warning the reader that the enemy had infiltrated education to sabotage our schools, should have prepared me for what was to come. Those who were familiar with the power struggle in the Party must have known what to expect, but I was totally taken aback when I arrived at the Institute on a Monday morning and saw the Military Police guarding the entrance. They let through some of my colleagues, but the rest of us were not allowed to enter. A man in a uniform briskly informed me that I was no longer working there. He told me to go home and await further communication. I was not even allowed to collect my belongings from my desk. For the moment, nobody was under arrest.

Where was M.? Somebody had seen him talking to the Military Police before he walked away in the direction of the Ring Road. My friends and I had no choice but to do the same. We telephoned M.'s wife, Vera, several times, only to learn that he had not arrived home. Had they taken him away? Would he have to publicly confess to his crimes like so many others? It was only in the evening that we learned that, without a second thought, he had gone to the dentist's.

It was a glorious Spring morning, and I had a whole day ahead of me with nothing to do. In spite of my anxieties, I was foolishly pleased, until an official letter arrived by post, terminating my contract. M. had still not been arrested. The *Free People* thundered against him, and his associates, who had tried to corrupt the educational system. He was an enemy of the People, which made him, and those connected to him, unsafe to know.

Being out of work was almost like a holiday. I was in no hurry to find a job, although it was illegal to be unemployed. Every citizen over school age had to work, including budding artists whose relatives would have been prepared to support them, and mothers after the end of their maternity leave. I had to find work of some kind soon, which would not be easy, because M. and his associates were banned from all white collar jobs. Factory workers were, presumably, less susceptible to contamination from Western ideas. I applied to several factories, but none of them were keen to employ a class enemy with no practical skills.

Lili, who knew how to sew, found shift-work in a clothes factory, but I was out of work for several weeks. It was nearly the middle of the summer when M.'s wife, Vera, rescued me from a potentially dangerous situation. She went to see an old flame of hers, who was now Chief Engineer of a large plant outside Budapest and begged him to employ me. The plant produced prefabricated slabs of concrete as building elements for tower blocks, and employed hundreds of workers. The Chief Engineer must have been a decent man because he did what Vera asked. He took one of his foremen aside and told him to let me have a job as an unskilled hand.

To earn a living, M. began to translate technical books from Russian. He became a frequent visitor to my flat, which offered better working conditions than the one he shared with his wife, his mother and his two young daughters. He usually arrived on the cogwheel tram in the morning armed with dictionaries and a portable typewriter and worked at the table, while I tiptoed in awe around him, producing meals out of thin air.

It was the craziest of summers. 'A little bit of dirt befits a girl,' M. was saying, 'but it shouldn't be on her face and neck. I find it charming that you never wash the soles of your feet.' I looked at my feet with embarrassment. Those days, I could walk barefoot on practically any surface (a legacy from the camps) so that I preferred not to wear shoes in the summer. It was true that I didn't give much attention to my soles, but why did he say that this was charming? I had been told often enough that I was untidy and careless of my clothes; now it seemed that my failings delighted M. He found it endearing that I forgot to check my new glasses after the tram stopped suddenly, which nearly knocked them out of my hands. 'Anybody else would have examined them immediately after arriving home,' he grinned, 'You're unique.' He liked the fact that I didn't know how to cook and looked at my abominable taste in decoration as a challenge. Something miraculous was taking place. I was no longer forgetful and untidy, but interesting and original. To my surprise and delight, M. found me attractive.

He would join me for walks, and would sit down on the hillside to listen to a lark. Stretching out in the tall grass under a cloudless sky, I was transformed into a dryad, Natasha Rostov, Manon Lescaut, a lizard sunning itself on a stone. I was no longer who I was, but the personification of everything desirable in a woman. Was it the scent of the pine trees, the humming of beetles in the tall grass, or the pressure of reality down in the city that caused this madness? This was how I learned that transformation, as told in myths and legends, was nothing less than the truth. It was no surprise to me that a frog could be changed into a prince, or a hunter into a stag. The ancient magic which had changed Daphne into a laurel tree was the same as the magic of the Summer of '51.

I do not know how other women are seduced but for me it has always been through the medium of words. Words transformed the Buda hill into Arcadia – and words changed my life again much later, at an age when I thought the time for enchantment was over. Then it was the power of poetry which created a new Spring and a lasting Summer for me. But that is a different story.

It was, I think, the end of June when my life as a labourer began. If I caught the first cogwheel tram at 5 a.m., I could arrive at work by seven. The factory was a grim place. As far as the eye could see, there was nothing but makeshift huts scattered on the sandy ground, noisy machines, and rows and rows of concrete slabs. Men carrying sacks on their backs queued in front of cement-mixers or fed the liquid concrete into stone troughs. The troughs had to be constantly agitated with the help of a sort of motorized pestle, similar to that which navvies use to pound wet concrete. My first job was to hold the handle of one of these, which shook my whole body, as if all my inner organs wanted loosening. Five minutes of this would have been hard, but a whole day? It was not really a job for a woman, but the People's Democracy didn't tolerate discrimination between the sexes. The *Free People* had proudly reported the introduction of women's brigades to coal mines and steel plants; therefore, they became obligatory everywhere. At a place where hundreds of men worked, there was one brigade with about a dozen tough girls from the neighbouring villages.

After a while, I couldn't hold the pounding pestle. I dropped it and waited for the foreman to come and see me. He asked me crossly what the trouble was; then told a man from a nearby brigade to take over. He beckoned me to follow him.

'Can you read numbers?' he asked.

'I can,' I said.

'Read this'. He pointed to a concrete slab between us with a row of numbers on it. He must have been impressed by the fact that I could read them even upside down, because for the rest of the day I had to copy numbers from slabs. My next job was to remove debris in a wheelbarrow.

I carried sacks of cement, shifted pebbles, and learned that hard labour hurts. In a day or two, the skin came off my palms. To my eternal shame, I offered a good skirt to the girl in the brigade for doing part of my job for me. 'She was used to it,' I later said defiantly to Lili, 'These girls were sent out to dig and hoe from the time they left school,' – forgetting that physical work must have been even harder for a child of twelve than it was for me.

Lili's job was not much easier than mine. Night shifts were as hard as getting up at 4.30 a.m. was for me. We usually spent Sundays together, listening to the radio, going for walks, and discovering that Sunday was the most boring day of the week.

'Why is it that you and I are the only ones without a boyfriend?' Lili moaned. 'Unattached men haven't been in existence since the war.'

'Let's phone around and see who we could invite,' I suggested. We consulted the directory in the telephone booth, but nobody we knew was likely to be free. Bother! At least, we were in the same boat, said Lili, which was a consolation. Anyhow, Lili had no right to complain. I was there when she had an argument with her last boyfriend, a medical student whom she would have loved to marry. I don't remember what the conversation was about – politics, most likely – but the ease with which Lili demolished her opponent's arguments, one by one. It was a brilliant performance. Had it been a duel, it would have ended with the young man lying mortally wounded on the floor, but then Lili would not have been so surprised to lose him.

Lili and I had cast each other in the role of *confidante,* in the manner of classic French drama, in which the protagonists express all their innermost thoughts and feelings to a friend. Had she known that I was hiding something from her, she would have been very hurt, yet living as I was, in a haze of elation, I didn't feel I was betraying her. Coming down from the hill was like switching worlds. At the end of the cogwheel tram was Arcadia; at the lower end, you changed to an ordinary tram which took you to work. How could I talk about it to anybody?

Yet it was I who ended it. I had no say about when and for how long I saw him. I thought that my heart would break when I did not ring him at the agreed time. I cried bitter tears when he finally rang me, and I did not respond. I had no rational explanation at the time: I only knew that I could not, I would not ring him. Not on those terms. No, even if my heart would break, no. One day I saw him on a bus: he smiled at me and I nearly fainted. I thought that no-one else had suffered like this.

I did not see him for several months, until one day, I suddenly felt the need to talk to him at once. I put on my coat and left the house to search the city for him. He could have been anywhere. He could have been at home, or visiting a friend, or drinking coffee in an 'espresso'. Disregarding the coffee houses in Buda, which he usually frequented, I walked like a somnambulist straight into the espresso in Pest where he was sitting next to a girl I knew. I opened the door and felt my way across the haze of cigarette smoke to his table, as if I was blind. He looked at me and stood up at once, murmuring some apology to the girl. He paid on the way out and we walked across the bridge to Buda, almost without a word. The cogwheel tram seemed to be waiting for us, as if it knew, as we did, that this was the last time.

I met him often after this (Budapest is small) but never on his own. It was four years, and many boyfriends later, when one day he sent word that he wanted to see me. I was in a bad state then, spectacularly suffering after a disastrous love affair, which had left me mad with anger and shame. I cried day and night and refused to see any of the friends who had witnessed the affair. My sister, Marinka, had no idea what to do with me. She gave me brandy and rum, refilling my glass with every bout of sobbing. Somebody's cousin in a distant town was willing to exchange her flat with mine for a fortnight and Marinka took me away, which was my salvation. It was on my return that M. sent a message concerning where and when he expected to meet me the next day.

It was a summons. I knew that he wanted to confront me with my hysterical behaviour, and I prepared a speech full of accusation and self pity.

M. pointed at a chair opposite himself. 'I was told that you had started to write something about literature for children. Tell me about it,' he commanded.

'I... I thought of writing about why we read novels,' I stammered, taken aback.

'Synopsis, please,' he said, 'What age-group?'

'I haven't decided yet,' I said, which he found unacceptable. He made me talk about age-groups and authors, and told me that he expected the first chapter within a month. Then, without a word, I was dismissed. When I left, my head was buzzing with plans for the book, which never materialized, but I felt better than I had done for weeks.

One never knows what the future brings. My life as an unskilled labourer would have been easier had I known that it was not for ever. It was M.'s wife, Vera, who again found me a job, as a 'conductor' in the Peto Institute.

Private enterprise did not exist, but the Institute of Mobility Rehabilitation was run by Andras Peto as if he owned it. The Institute was built, furnished and staffed entirely according to the specifications of Peto, who employed and dismissed whom he wanted, without any interference; he was even allowed to have a say in the choice of the Institute's belligerent, but exceedingly stupid, Party Secretary. Peto could do anything because, according to rumor, somebody high up in the Party hierarchy was supporting him.

Peto refused to have qualified nurses, child carers, teachers, or any other professional working for him, and he required no formal qualifications from the young women he interviewed to work with him. They had to be bright and physically strong, with no preconceived ideas about disability. As far as possible, he chose girls who had a boyfriend and a harmonious family life, dismissing anyone who said she wanted to sacrifice her life to 'poor crippled children'. A new 'conductor' received no special training, but joined the others in washing, feeding, instructing, and consoling the children, and doing, with them, the exercises specified by Peto.

Looking back at life in the newly built one-storey building in Buda, the most arresting thing about it was the total absence of orthopaedic aids. No calipers, crutches, or wheelchairs, as if it were not the home of physically disabled children and adults. The sunny central therapy room was surrounded by ten rooms with nothing in them but bunk beds. The beds were made to Peto's specification and could be easily stacked up to make room for exercises. They had no mattresses but horizontal wooden slats covered with a blanket which were surprisingly comfortable. I can testify to this, as I slept on them for years when on night duty. There was neither a dining room, nor a recreation room, nor a schoolroom, since every waking hour was taken up with exercises. The exercises were directed by the 'conductors'. In order to be available during the night, the 'conductors' worked alternating shifts. Polio victims, as well as those with neurological motor diseases, moved around, holding the slotted cross bars on the backs of the chairs, or sat on the floor, repeating the same movement over and over again. Monotonous chanting, and a slow counting to five, filled the building all day.

I have often been asked for the secret of its spectacular success. The answer was Peto himself, a fat taciturn Buddha, whom I never saw smiling and who never said 'thank you' to anyone. He would often emerge from his office at the side of the building to wander around and supervise the exercises, altering the sequence or adding another movement. He seldom talked to the 'conductors' directly, but left it to his deputy, Maria Hary, a young doctor obsessed by her adoration of Peto. His force of character permeated the Institute, so that a new movement in a finger was a sensation, and nothing in the world was more important than that Annie had stood erect and unaided, or that Peter had taken two steps on his own.

Nothing in the world, indeed, could be more important than this, which I understood at once. Who would not, on seeing bright and beautiful Christa flailing her arms and legs in the grip of a hideous neurological impairment, or looking at the face of a four year old boy whose two legs had become dangling attachments to his body, as a result of recent polio? Peto almost seemed to absorb each individual's disability into his own body and knew the strength and weakness of every muscle within them. Did he ever think of anything other than the next exercise for each? Under pressure from the Ministry, he would occasionally give a lecture to the assembled 'conductors' but nothing could be learned from it. He mumbled incoherently, and what he said made no sense to us. Although he explained nothing, everyone understood what to do. Education? Play? There was no time for these. Even the youngest child would not have exchanged one unaided step for a whole toy shop.

The lack of formal education did not appear to affect the children's intellectual development. You have to take my word for it, because Peto would no more tolerate a psychologist with an intelligence test than a salesman peddling orthopaedic aids. Exercise was education. As far as I know, none of the children had any difficulty with learning when they went back to school.

For various reasons, Peto's innovations could not be fully maintained after his death. Three of them were, I believe, crucial: the constant presence of the same people; exercise in groups with a conductor, rather than alone; and the repetitive use of *rhythm*. Peto was no miracle worker but he tapped deep-seated human needs. The constant presence of the same people created a closed-in world of 'us' which the coming and going of teachers, counsellors and physiotherapists would have diluted. As to the rhythmical chanting of people working together, it is probably as old as the pyramids. So are the rhymes which children chant spontaneously in their group games, and I suspect that the old method of reading from the blackboard in unison was more successful than today's educationalists are willing to admit.

Soon after I began work there, I found it difficult to talk about anything other than the Institute. How could outsiders get bored with my minute rendering of an exercise which resulted in a step forward? Anyone at the Institute would have understood it, even those who were suspicious of the political pariahs Peto employed. Myra's husband was in prison, Isabella was a baroness, Paul was a 'defrocked' doctor. I began my career as an alien when, on being requested to put comments on the pin-board, I composed a humorous ditty about an imaginary dormitory room which I called Room X. It was met by an icy silence from the other 'conductors'.

'What made you attack poor Magda?' shouted one of them when I begged her to tell me what I had done.

'Why ask me? You know very well. You've poked fun at Room 10. They've sworn never to talk to you again,' she said. Of course! The dormitories in the Institute were marked with Roman numerals. I tried to explain the concept of X as a symbol of an unknown quantity, but no-one believed me.

The Party Secretary, who was also the caretaker, was particularly suspicious. 'I know that you were at that Institute of Education,' she said, 'What did you do there?'

'Well, we produced school books. I collected material...'

'Collected material? That means spying! Have you been a spy?'

As a result, I did not dare refuse her when she wanted me to teach Russian. Somebody in authority became aware that there was no Russian language class at the Institute and the omission had to be urgently remedied. It was no use telling her that I did not speak a word of Russian. I had to teach, and teach I did. I got hold of a beginner's book and hastily memorized the Cyrillic alphabet for the first lesson. The Russian language class progressed nicely since the yawning 'conductors' could not care less that I was never more than one lesson ahead of them.

Although I was deeply involved with the patients, I never became like some of the 'conductors', who grew into the fabric of the place and would never be able to do anything else. Even after two years, I could not leave for home without suffocating guilt. Neither could I get used to shift work. I scrubbed floors and emptied potties and made life-long friendships, but it was not through choice that I worked there. It was a better job than Lili's work at the factory, but I would gladly have left it if I could.

Aranka - a story.

The Russian language lessons folded up after a visit by a friendly inspector who spoke the language, but the workers had to be educated, and I was given the task of running the obligatory seminars on 'Marxism-Leninism.' Since my degree was fairly recent, and my belief in Marx unshaken, I was looking forward to sharing my enjoyment of understanding difficult concepts with the other 'conductors'. We began with 'Das Kapital' which, I was told, Marx had written for the workers.

A girl, who had recently been appointed to the Institute, interrupted me. 'What does the word "category" mean?' she asked.

A question at last! Her name was Aranka. She was a sturdy girl with a squareish body and a freckled face. She sounded genuinely interested.

'Category means… how shall I put it? Take, for example, the word "furniture". Furniture is something you have never seen. You have seen a table, a chair, a wardrobe, and so on. But "furniture" is an abstraction which covers them all. Or take another example, "animal". You can see a bird, or a dog, a lizard but not an "animal" which is an abstraction. We call these umbrella terms "categories".'

'But then the word "bird" must also be a category because it is an umbrella term for finches, storks and blackbirds,' said Aranka.

'Absolutely right!' I cried, 'You are going down from the abstract to the concrete. "Finch", "stork", and "blackbird" are umbrella words for the individual birds.'

We carried on with 'Das Kapital,' but Aranka was not listening. A little later she wanted to know something else. 'Can you put the categories themselves into a category?'

'Of course,' I said, delighted, 'Furniture, cutlery, books, and many others terms, come under the category of "object". Animals and plants come under the category of "living things".'

'This is what I thought,' Aranka nodded. 'So which is the category on the top which covers all the others?'

'According to the Greek philosopher, Aristotle, who first wrote about this, there are ten. These are quantity, quality, relation, place, time... I don't remember the others, but I'll look it up and tell you next time.'

I managed to sit next to her during the midday meal. 'Where did you work before you came here?' I asked.

'I was in service,' she answered curtly.

'But not all of the time, surely? What did you do before that?'

'What is it to you? I was a domestic. I was a domestic all my life.' It was only later, when we became friends, that I pieced together her past. Aranka had been a foundling, brought up by a peasant family which fostered wards of the state. She attended the village school where the clothes provided for orphans singled her out. At the age of fourteen, she went into service with a childless couple in Budapest, and stayed with them for four years.

'They weren't cruel, or anything like that, but...they didn't see me. On hot summer days, for instance, they would walk stark naked through the house, as if I was a piece of furniture.'

But they had books and Aranka read whatever she could put her hands on. The wife of her next employer, or the one after that, provided her with school books, or was it the priest? I only remember what followed next. The brother of her last employer, who was a frequent visitor to the house, fell in love with Aranka. It was he who found her a place to live and a job at the Peto Institute. The story had the makings of a romance, but not for Aranka, who thought him weak, and did not want anything to do with him. 'I've told him that he's pathetic, yet he wants to marry me. Huh!'

I imagined the man to be old and ugly but he was, in fact, a good looking dentist in his late thirties. I often saw him hovering around the Institute waiting for Aranka but he only talked to me when Aranka realised that her lodgings cost more than the rent she was paying. She was furious. Albert – I think his name was Albert – tried to enlist me on his side. 'But I don't want him to support me,' Aranka cried, 'even if I have to sleep at the railway station.'

'Come and stay with me,' I offered, 'the mattress on the sofa makes a quite comfortable second bed.' Aranka collected her sparse belongings and moved in. My stance as Aranka's self-appointed teacher did not last long, because I had to admit that she was sharper and more tenacious than me. She was a Party member and read voraciously in the Marxist literature. Albert, the lovelorn dentist, was soon relegated to the past.

A flat in the Buda hills was a magnet for my friends and acquaintances in the summer. They would arrive unannounced, bringing with them coffee, or a freshly baked loaf, or a French cheese from a secret source, and we would talk. How we talked! Arguments and emotional appeals were tossed like volley balls across the room. Aranka usually sat and listened.

'I'll tell you the latest political joke,' said Peter, who lived with his wife and their baby in one room in the house, 'It's about the young polar bear who turns to his mother and says, 'Whatever you tell me, Mum, I'm cold.'

Everybody laughed except Aranka for whom the Communist Paradise did not seem cold at all. She was cross because Peter had inadvertently dropped an ashtray belonging to her which had smashed to pieces. Peter had picked up the pieces and apologized.

'It doesn't matter,' I said, 'It was only an ashtray. Forget it.'

Aranka jumped up angrily, 'On the contrary, it does matter. The ashtray was mine.' She turned to me, 'How could you say that? I do mind, and don't care whether I'm not supposed to say so.'

We were all taken aback and looked at each other. This was not how one should behave. The only thing to do was to talk quickly about something else.

One of the achievements of the People's Republic was to open up further education for the children of workers and peasants. Anyone whose father was a manual labourer, or who tilled the land, could now go to grammar school and university. Massively discriminating against middle class children and the children of professionals, the new colleges pushed and cajoled poorly educated and often unwilling youngsters towards professional careers. Many were successful, like the boy who later became my friend Magda's son in law. He would never have gone to grammar school without this social engineering, which would have been a loss to many people. Aranka, of course, was cut out for such education. She applied for college and was accepted at once. At the end of her introductory year, she was advised to study law. After a three year's crash course, she became a 'people's judge', presiding over relatively small breaches of the law.

Her college was in a town some distance from Budapest, and with all the subsequent upheavals of my life, we lost touch. I often wondered what had happened to her. It was after the suppression of the '56 revolution that I saw Aranka again.

After much hesitation, I had decided to leave the country. I was sitting in Marinka's kitchen discussing the next step, when the bell rang. To my amazement, it was Aranka. I was delighted to see her, but it crossed my mind that this was no ordinary visit. Communist officials had been violently attacked by enraged mobs during the Revolution; had she come to ask for help? But no, the Revolution was over and power had been restored to those who had it previously. Retaliation had already begun. Aranka, however, looked neither satisfied nor victorious. Her face was drawn, her clothes shabbier than ever. She looked much older than her years; she looked broken.

'I was looking for you in your flat but you'd moved, from which I deduced that you'd followed the crowd flooding out of the country and so I decided to ask your sister about you,' she said.

'Aranka! I can hardly believe it's you. I had no address. You'd disappeared. Where do you live?'

'In a village at the back of nowhere. You wouldn't know it. It is a five hour journey by train. I had to come to Budapest on official business but I'm going back tonight. Are you going to leave the country?'

Crossing the border to Austria was, by then, a dangerous undertaking. The border guards and the land mines were back in place. A member of the judiciary was the last person with whom to discuss such a flight, but this was Aranka.

'I am going to leave in a few days. Everything is settled. It's such luck that you came today because once I'd gone abroad, we'd never find each other again. Tell me! Tell me about yourself. Your career as a judge. What are you doing in that village?'

'I'm living there, in a hovel without running water or electricity. And I'm no longer a judge. I've left the judiciary and of course I am no longer in the Party either.'

Good grief! I'd never met anybody who had actually renounced her Party membership. The repercussions must have been terrifying. But Aranka said that after a while she could no longer bear to sentence people whom she knew had committed no real crime. Three years for a factory worker who had taken home a hammer, as a warning to the others; five years for sabotage when production faltered; sentencing former small-holders for not having declared the grain in the loft. Aranka was dealing with everyday cases which the papers never reported.

'Aranka, come with us. You can start a new life anywhere. I know a route which is fairly safe.'

'Oh no! I've been a part of this. I helped to make it and I benefited from it. I won't run away. Besides, I have a child.'

'And you never told me! A boy or a girl? How old? Did you get married?'

Aranka sat with her shoulders hunched, sinking into herself. Her voice was harsh when she answered,

'It is called hydrocephalus, water on the brain. The symptoms are a grossly enlarged head, epileptic fits and idiocy. He is eight months old. Shall I tell you what it feels like when somebody bends smiling over the pram and then looks away, horrified? My heart breaks when I see other mothers walking their children.'

'Oh, Aranka, my dear Aranka.' I tried to embrace her. 'I wish I could do something... but I'm leaving the country. Why didn't you tell me before? Will you give me your address? Please!'

Aranka shook her head in denial and began silently to cry. I never saw or heard of her again.

7

Aunt Helen was still living in one room in what used to be her elegant flat in Hajós Street. Uncle Marci's chemist shop had been nationalised. Had he not committed suicide as a persecuted Jew, he would have been stripped of everything he had, as a class enemy. Aunt Helen tried to peddle shoes, and then she got a lowly job in the shop which used to be hers. She was in her fifties, and now – in middle age – had become a tall, handsome woman, despite the squint which had always disfigured her self-esteem. The bourgeois surroundings, which she had built up around her with such great effort, had collapsed. The Persian rugs, the silver and the china had gone, even Uncle Marci's hand-written diploma with the scroll and seal had disappeared while she was in hiding. She was on her own. I'd turned out painfully differently from what she had wanted, and there wasn't even a little maid to confide in, or order about.

Of all this I understood nothing. I kept a nightgown and a toothbrush in her room and bedded down on the mattress whenever it was too late to catch the cogwheel tram, accepting casually any food that was in the house. She didn't understand what I was doing with my life. Nearly thirty and still not married was even worse than my attachment to unsuitable men. She cautiously tried to reach out to me, but I looked at her with the unseeing eye of the adolescent, for whom she remained the fiend who had magically ousted her mother.

On a Sunday morning in April, she came to see me in my flat on the hill and we went for a walk. It was a sunny day but a strong wind was chasing the clouds, so that I lent her a headscarf and a large woollen shawl to put round her shoulders.

We walked to the Red Star Hotel and the open country behind it. The meadow was ours, provided we avoided the large brick building which everybody called *The Convent* further down the hill. It was, of course, no longer a convent since convents and monasteries had been dismantled long ago. Now there was a wall around the building, with barbed wire on its outer perimeter. According to rumours, it was one of the interrogation centres of the dreaded State Police. It was some distance from the houses on the hill, so that nobody heard or saw what was going on inside. Had somebody told me that in a few month's time I'd see it for myself, I would not have believed it.

On the way back, the colour of the sky began to change rapidly and become nearly black. We had to bend forward to fight the wind which was no longer friendly. It blew into our eyes, making Aunt Helen's borrowed blanket flop around her. She pulled down her headscarf to cover the escaping strands of her grey hair and held on to my arm for support.

A young woman was struggling up the hill from the opposite direction, sheltering her small daughter with her arm against the wind. The child noticed Aunt Helen.

'Mummy, look, the witch! There is the witch!' She was dancing excitedly, pointing at Aunt Helen, while her embarrassed mother tried to shush her. I cannot believe that I sniggered. I looked at Aunt Helen who had flushed with shame and hurt and had tears in her eyes.

8

Stalin's death in March 1953 shook the whole of Eastern Europe. Wasn't he immortal? His face beamed from the walls of every office, schoolroom, lobby and concert hall, radiating honesty and benevolence. His presence seemed eternal.

There is a short story by a Hungarian writer about a famous doctor who is approached by Death himself, asking to have his life saved. Death, in the story, is very old and sick and needs an operation. Should the doctor operate or let Death die, thereby saving the rest of mankind? Being a conscientious surgeon he decides to operate but, in spite of his efforts, he fails to save his patient. This, however, is of no consequence. Death, the old man's son, takes over and continues his father's work.

People could hardly talk of anything else. Who is this Khrushchev? Would there be any changes in Hungary as a result? There was a palpable turbulence within the government, and the waves reached the newspapers and radio. There was hope in the air, but there was also a surprising amount of unthinking grief. Even people whose lives had been undermined by the regime reacted by bursting into tears. The archetypal image of the Father was stronger than common sense. Millions were grieving for a symbolic father, much as millions would later grieve for a princess in England who symbolized youth and grace for them.

The invisible noose around our necks seemed a little looser. In this atmosphere of uncertainty, I might even get a white-collar job. The problem, however, was how to find one. I plucked up courage and went to see M.

'Do something!' I pleaded. 'Please do something. I can't stand it much longer in the Peto Institute.'

It was a shameless request since he himself was slaving as an unofficial translator, ghosting for former friends, many of whom pocketed half the fees. He telephoned the writer Géza Hegedűs, the Head of the Literature Department at the School of Dramatic Arts, whom he had known of old, and asked for his help. Since I had never read literature at University, I cannot imagine how he managed to get Hegedűs to support my application for a job as his assistant but, to my amazement, he did. I was told to fill out a form, produce a CV, and was accepted as an assistant lecturer without further ado. The procedure was not unusual at a time when a politically reliable mechanic could, overnight, become the factory's managing director.

The School of Dramatic Arts! I oscillated between panic and elation. It was late in July and the term started in October. The task ahead of me was similar to when I was six and went home from school to tell my mother that I had to learn all the multiplication tables for the next day. My anxious mother, who had immense respect for learning but knew nothing of elementary education, sat down to listen to me after the evening meal. By midnight, we were both in tears. My mother, with a cold compress on her aching head, persevered, as if my future educational career depended on seven times eight. It was only after midnight that she gave up on her retarded child and we went to bed. And now I had less than two months to prepare myself for the job.

I rushed to the central Public Library near the National Museum to borrow a 'Short History of European Literature,' which I'd leafed through as a teenager. What did they mean by 'short?' Six hundred pages at least, and that without the actual books. From 'A' for Aeschylus to 'Z' for Zola, with special attention given to contemporary Soviet literature, which I was most likely to teach. Never mind Soviet literature, I had not even read 'War and Peace' and knew Shakespeare only from the theatre. The Greeks, thank God, seemed only to have written plays with few characters; Virgil we had done at school, but who was Torquato Tasso? I heaved my suitcase full of books onto the cogwheel tram and settled down to read. I must have read for about fourteen hours a day, and only emerged for air when I realised half-way through why Goncharov's 'Oblomov' was so familiar. I had read it the week before.

I would not have been so desperate had I known my future boss. Géza Hegedűs would not have dreamed of expecting more from a person than they could give. He was a rubicund, jovial, darling man, who laughed and talked a great deal, and never knowingly did anyone any harm. He was hopelessly untidy, despite the efforts of his equally apple-shaped wife, whom he adored. His lectures were immensely entertaining, packed with factual details, which he delivered without notes. He had a phenomenal memory, and did not mind being used as a walking encyclopedia.

'I had a phone call yesterday,' he told me at our customary coffee-break in the nearby espresso, 'and an agitated voice asked me some details concerning cartography in fourteenth century Portugal. I advised him to contact the Academy of Science. "But it's from there that I'm phoning you!" was the answer.'

Hegedűs was a prolific novelist. According to college lore, he was in possession of a typewriter which had two funnels inserted into the keyboard. He would pour black coffee into one, rum into the other, get it going, and a new historical novel for older children would be on its way. He was a born story-teller, colourful, interesting, and only rarely inaccurate. I followed him to his lectures like a shadow, whilst devouring quantities of indigestible Soviet novels because I was soon to teach Soviet Literature to folk dancers.

Literature was taught at a high academic level to students of dramaturgy. The demands were almost equally high on film makers and actors. Folk dancers, the darlings of Communist public entertainment, needed however, mainly health and stamina, and their educational attainments were rarely questioned. They had probably been attached to the Drama School under duress. Hegedűs must have been pleased to get a minion to teach them Soviet propaganda novels.

After a year or two I went on to lecture on European drama as well to the folk dancers, and Soviet literature to the rest. I could not ask for more. I had an extra income from deputising for Hegedűs at the external lectures which were part of the educational project for working men and women. Not only was education free at all levels, reprints of classics and books in general were also heavily subsidised, and theatre and opera tickets were distributed in factories for almost nothing. Countless people must have benefited from this, even though many theatre seats remained empty because the tired workers had no inclination to use them.

'They've scheduled a talk on poetry at this working girls' hostel for Saturday. Would you like to do it?' Hegedűs asked me. These extramural talks were extremely well paid.

'Whose poetry?' I asked.

'Oh, I don't know. Poetry in general. I don't think that those girls know many poems. Up to you.'

I duly arrived at the hostel on Saturday evening, armed with a thick volume of *Seven Hundred Years of Hungarian Poetry*. My reception was not just cool, but downright hostile. Saturday was the only evening in a six-day working week when the girls could have gone out without having to think of the alarm clock going off next morning. I had no idea where to begin. The boldest of them said that she hated poetry.

'Do you like dance music?' I asked. Of course they did. They knew dozens of tunes and lyrics I had never heard of, and were ready to sing.

> *Her hair was gold, like ripe corn in the meadow, her mouth was sweet like sugared pineapple...*It was one of the hits of the day.

'Wait a minute,' I said, opening my book. 'Here is a poem by Gyula Juhász. Listen:

> *The precise gold of her hair, I don't remember,*
> *I only know that meadows may be gold,*
> *When cornfields ripen just before September,*
> *There's something of her colouring in the fold.*

I remember that evening very well because it was one of my rare successes. They were hungry for words about sadness and parting, hope and despair, and saw that the lyrics of the dance music were flat and banal. They listened to the poems as if I had uncovered a secret they had never known.

I also remember the seven hundredth anniversary of Dante's birth when the howling wind filled my mouth with snow as I waited for the tram to take me to Csepel. Somebody high up in the hierarchy felt that the plant's many hundreds of workers should not be deprived of hearing about the great man's life and work. Hegedűs had good reason to transfer the honour to me.

The plant was huge, and I was sloshed with snow and mud by the time I found the House of Culture and the comrade responsible for educational projects.

'Yes, yes, of course. Dante, I know,' he said when I introduced myself. 'Would you mind going into this cubicle and waiting? I'll be with you in a jiffy.'

The cubicle was curtained off from a larger area and the music coming through the curtain was ominous. But the comrade was as good as his word. He reappeared, pulled away the curtain, and led me courteously to a table and chair in the middle of what I realised was a stage. I found myself sitting in front of a cinema screen, facing an audience of several hundred people who began to clap and whistle when they saw me.

'Dante Alghieri was an Italian,' I began when I found my voice, 'He was the author of the *Divine Comedy* which...' But the noise of the departing audience stifled me.

'Don't worry,' whispered the Cultural Representative, 'they'll come back after the interval. We're showing a Western.'

My friendly, sunlit office became a meeting place and a sort of advisory centre for students. It was there that I regularly guided Heidi through her re-sits after she failed her exams.

To look at Heidi reminded one of fairy tales in which the princess was so beautiful that '*one could sooner look at the sun than at her'*. She was also talented and had a good singing voice, so that the staff bent backwards to overlook her fathomless stupidity. 'I can't let her pass,' said Hegedűs, crossly, after her oral, 'You do it!'

What would be a good question to put to her? I tried to decide which of the ancient Greek playwrights most deserved to be misunderstood by Heidi. But first we had to clarify an important point. 'How come that Sophocles was born in 496 BC, yet it was 386 BC when he died?'

'I've often wondered about it myself,' she pouted, 'but I still don't know.'

'I tell you what. I'm going to recite a short poem by Sappho and you tell me what it's about:

Dear mother, my spinning wheel is stilled.
Great Aphrodite has conquered me.
A lover, a lover is what I want!'

Heidi pondered this. Not for nothing had she been a young Pioneer at school, however. 'The poem says that in ancient Greece girls were exploited in factories,' she explained.

What became of her? Unlike many students whose names are well known to this day, Heidi's career must have sunk into oblivion as soon as her legendary beauty began to fade. I'd like to think that a rich man married her and that she lived happily ever after. But the rich men of the day were Party officials, clinging precariously to their mansions and chauffeur-driven cars. They would want to marry into the family of machine operators or steel workers. Poor Heidi!

Appointment to the School of Dramatic Arts was probably the best thing that ever happened to me. I was reading furiously and systematically all the time and eventually climbed the academic ladder to some degree of seniority. When circumstances made me return to Psychology, I benefited at least as much from Balzac and Tolstoy, as I ever learned from experimental research.

The hallmark of a true friend is that she sticks with you even when you have good luck. My appointment to the Drama School did not affect my friendship with Lili, who was still slaving in the rag trade. Her family moved out of Budapest to the suburb of Kispest, but she could not change her job, and had to travel to work for two hours both ways. Was it she, or someone else, who casually mentioned the life-sized dummy representing Uncle Sam in the lobby? It was placed under the clock wearing a striped suit and top hat decorated with the stars and stripes, and those who arrived late for work had to shake its hand, saying, 'I'm your friend.' Being late strengthened the powers of the capitalist enemy and made you a traitor to the peace effort. Tyranny made us into children.

9

In the aftermath of Stalin's death, tiny cracks began to appear in the icy monolith, followed by a small earthquake, that is, the XXth Congress of the Soviet Communist Party at which Khrushchev disclosed the truth about Stalin's show trials. Our own Mátyás Rákosi, Stalin's greatest Hungarian disciple, retired on the advice of his Soviet friends, and Imre Nagy became Prime Minister. The Party's grip on the printed word eased, and poets and writers, traditionally the custodians of the nation's conscience, began to have their voices heard. The students of the Drama School openly criticised censorship, and Zsuzsa Simon, the Communist Head of the School, was uncertain how far she should allow these dissenting voices to be heard.

The Party's trust in Zsuzsa's loyalty had been recently proved by granting her an exit visa to attend a conference on school television in Paris. On her return, she was duty bound to call a staff conference to report on the conference. We heard about television. I had even seen a set in the radio broadcasting studio when a silly little play of mine was being rehearsed. It was a large box which, if switched on, began to buzz and show rapidly moving white lines across the screen. It wasn't very impressive, although I was told that such a box could transmit pictures and was used as a sort of home cinema in Western countries.

'School television is an evil invention, Comrades,' Zsuzsa told us, 'If it gets off the ground it could replace teachers, with lessons broadcast simultaneously to all schools. The idea, of course, is to brainwash French children with centrally devised programmes, in order to make them willing subjects for exploitation.'

After appropriate comments from her audience, Zsuzsa closed the meeting. Everyone left, apart form her close friends, who pulled their chairs nearer to her. I had left with the others but had to return to ask something of Hegedűs, who motioned me to sit down. I caught the end of Zsuzsa's true report ' ...and when they led us across a courtyard at the back of the building I saw a bucket with a rag for mopping up. *It was made of nylon,*' she said in awe, 'Man-made fibres are so common they use them as floor-cloths!'

Man-made fibres were not unknown to me since there was a time, after the war, when people could travel abroad and foreign parcels could be sent. I had heard of men's shirts which needed no ironing, but dripped dry by themselves after washing and of nylon stockings which did not ladder. Some of my male acquaintances babbled about robots and computer technology, to which I paid little attention. A ban on foreign travel meant that one would never see such curiosities for oneself.

Was never visiting Paris again too high a price for the land reform which benefited 65,00 peasants; for opening up higher education to those who could not access it before; for a society where a manual labourer could hold up his head, knowing that the country belonged to him? If only they hadn't ruined it by forced collectivisation, impossible demands on productivity, and show trials! Only now was it possible to debate such things.

The first critical words on Stalin opened up discussions which would previously have been unthinkable. It would have been equally unthinkable for students to organise a protest march on October 23, 1956, as they did in sympathy with a recent uprising in Poland.

It should have been on a day in March, when the fresh wind melting the ice heralds the coming of spring, rather than a day in October. The students from the Drama School walked four abreast towards the statue of the poet Petőfi, who had died fighting the Austrians during the revolution of 1848. The march was swollen by workers from the suburbs, and by people who joined it off the streets, as it passed. Traffic stopped and everyone began to sing. Other protest marches emerged from every direction, like the tributaries of a great river meandering towards the Danube, all of them converging on the statue. A promise of future happiness pervaded the crowd, as if a change of government would be also a guarantee against grief, bad luck and unrequited love.

The group next to me suddenly broke into a nationalistic song, which I hadn't heard since the end of the war, about the restitution of a Greater Hungary. I was startled. I had hoped never to hear this song again. It had strong fascist undertones, since Hungary had joined the Germans mainly because Hitler had promised to restore to it the territories lost to Hungary after the First World War. Patriotism had somehow become equated with fascism.

'It's still a puzzle to me,' said my colleague, Ibi, half a century later, 'why you suddenly broke into the *Internationale*, to everyone's surprise.'

'Did I? Yes, you're right. I remember now. I quite surprised myself, as well,' I replied.

After all, the march was a protest against our Soviet overlords, and, just as nobody had dared to sing the *Internationale* under the pre-war fascist regime, nobody had, as yet, dared to sing a semi-fascist song under the Soviet regime.

'I see,' Ibi said, 'you thought that communism restricted your life, but that fascism wanted to take it away.'

Did freedom mean that fascism would return as soon as the state ceased to oppress it? It has taken me decades of living in Britain to understand that what an ideology or political system wishes to achieve is less important than *how it deals with dissent.* In truth, I hadn't been *thinking* at all. Politics may seem to be seated in our brains, but, when it comes to the crunch, it emerges from our guts.

The rest of that day, and the days that followed, passed in a blur. Students jumped onto Soviet tanks, trying to persuade the Russian soldiers not to shoot. Soldiers of the Hungarian army handed over their weapons to the crowd. An outburst of popular rage toppled the huge Stalin statue, and people rushed to hack it to pieces. Lorries and horse-drawn carts arrived from the countryside to distribute food freely. I saw watches and bracelets untouched in a jeweller's shop, with a piece of paper stuck on the broken window: 'The revolutionary does not steal.'

I was somewhere else when unarmed people were shot in front of the radio building, and when the massacre took place in Parliament Square, so that it was only later that I pieced together the events of those thirteen glorious days. There was fighting on the streets, from the rooftops and doorways, while agitated politicians bargained behind closed doors, and a Soviet envoy arrived. It was mostly students and teenagers who did the fighting. Radio Free Europe sent special messages to those youngsters who couldn't get hold of a weapon: 'Fill a bottle with petrol, stick paper into it, and throw it out of the window at the jeeps', it advised, 'Lard and cooking oil on sloping pavements slow down tanks.' The two boys I met on my way home must have been still at school. They were carrying a heavy rifle between them.

'We don't know what to do with it,' the older of the two told me, 'and Mum would kill us if we took it home.'

In the midst of all of this, I received an urgent message from my brother-in law, Dani, asking me to see him. I was intrigued. My sister was in hospital for a minor operation and Dani hadn't been on talking terms with me since my childhood. What did he want? I went to their house at once.

Dani opened the door unsmilingly, and ushered me into the living room. A heavily built young man got up from an armchair to greet me. 'I'm sure you remember Tibi,' Dani said.

Tibi of all people! Of course, I remembered Tibi, though I hadn't recognised him immediately. He was Dani's nephew, the prodigal son of his sister, whom I hadn't seen since we were children. He had been the only boy in the family, and the centre of my pre-adolescent day-dreams when we moved to St Lőrinc. I hadn't seen him since, and had only heard that he'd suffered terribly from eczema, and had spent half his life in hospital, with his arms tied down to prevent him scratching himself. Later, he had been apprenticed as a dental technician, but had then run away from home and became a communist. It was such a terrible thing to do that the adults spoke about it almost in whispers. At the time, he was not only endangering his own life, but possibly that of his parents. He became the black sheep of the family, which had presumably changed when the communists came to power, and Tibi had become a major in the dreaded State Security system. I hadn't heard of him again, until his mother died and Dani attended her funeral. According to my sister, Tibi had arrived at the graveside in uniform, flanked by two bodyguards. He had stood there for a few moments and then, without greeting any of his relatives, had driven off in a large black car. Now here he was, standing in the middle of the room, hat in hand, and smiling.

'Tibi has come here, because has nowhere else to go,' Dani said, 'He tells me his life's in danger. He had only an office job, but some of the crowd have gone wild, and they lynch anyone who worked for State Security. I've told him he can't stay here, but you live alone, so you could hide him.'

'I had nothing to do with any of the atrocities,' Tibi said, 'I've only been working in an office. I know this could be dangerous, but if you refuse to help me, I'm lost.' I too had heard that a man wearing the dreaded State Security uniform had been hanged from a lamp post. Even if Tibi had played no part in intimidation and torture, he would be in no position to prove that when confronted by an angry crowd.

And why should it be dangerous to hide him? The Revolution would surely succeed. The Russians were leaving the country, and life would never be dangerous again.

'I'm nobody's judge,' I said, 'You can stay with me until you sort something out.'

To Dani's visible relief, we left the house together. Tibi pulled his hat down over his forehead, and didn't say much all the way to my flat. He stayed for almost a week until, mysteriously, he received a message to say it was safe for him to leave. I later heard that he had been able to cross the border into Austria with the tens of thousands of others who were fleeing the country.

I had no difficulty in introducing Tibi to those friends who also lived on Freedom Hill, and frequently popped in to discuss the latest news. They, too, were upset by the lynching, and accepted what Tibi told them. He stayed indoors most of the time, while I went to the Drama School where there were no classes, but people were milling in and out to hear the latest news, and to find out whether the canteen was still open.

The Revolutionary Students' Council faced a dilemma. They had seized the Party Secretary's dossiers, and a heated debate started on what should be done with them. There was a dossier on everyone in the country. They contained information on which a person's career, a spouse's job, or a child's acceptance at grammar school, might depend. Dossiers were based largely on the reports of informers, who might have overheard a careless remark, or have drawn a person into an argument.The informants themselves were spied upon by others, who didn't dare refuse, in case they themselves became suspect. Everyone knew this, but to read one's dossier - and to discover that a trusted friend or colleague had reported one's words to the Party Secretary (even though one might have done the same thing) - would have burst the fabric of social relations like a bomb. One didn't have to be a member of the

Party to act as an informant, but the comrades must have thought me too scatterbrained, since I had never been approached. But although I had no sympathy with those who reported on me, I knew that opening Pandora's box would have disastrous consequences. Some of the students understood this; others insisted on knowing the truth.

'Hamlet must have faced this problem too,' I said to the Revolutionary Council. 'Having travelled from civilized Wittenberg to barbaric Denmark, he faced the dilemma whether or not to seek out the truth, and punish the guilty – or do nothing. He would probably have distributed the dossiers.'

'Are you suggesting that we should do the same?'

'No, I'm not. Hamlet obeyed the Voice and, as a result, the stage becomes littered with corpses – of the innocent, as well as the guilty. I think the files should be burned.'

'And never know who one's enemies are? It's an outrageous suggestion!'

But, if fascism had taught me anything, it was not to take part in the lethal chain of revenge and counter-revenge. The question whether I was right or wrong, however, was to remain unanswered. When the Russian tanks returned, the Party Secretary retrieved the dossiers.

Tibi was the ideal house guest. He pulled a mattress onto the landing to sleep on, fetched the milk every morning, helped with the household chores, and made knowledgeable comments when, glued to the radio my friends and I debated the situation. Would the Russians return? It was unthinkable that the country's plight should be disregarded by the West, that the flower of the country's young should have died in vain. The will of the people seemed to have swept away the corrupt and dithering government, but the country's fate was still undecided.

History, as I know, is red in tooth and claw, but it can have its farcical moments. The news that Russian tanks were re-entering Hungary was contradicted by the latest information. We were anxiously listening to the radio when my friend and neighbour, Peter, laughed out loud.

'Peter, have you gone mad?'

'No, but I've just remembered the story of the village lad who stood before the magistrate, accused of raping Mariska. The magistrate was surprised: 'But Joska, he said, 'you've always been a decent lad. How come you did such a terrible thing?' 'Well, your honour,' said Joska, shamefacedly, 'it was like this. It was a hot day and I spotted Mariska asleep under a haystack with her skirt over her face. My evil self said, wouldn't it be nice to fuck her, but my better self protested, you mustn't do it, Joska. It would be easy, my evil self argued. You would never do such a thing, my better self retorted. And, you see, your honour, while these two were arguing, I just fucked her.'

I couldn't believe that the Soviet troops, which had just left the country, would return. We knew that our fate was being debated throughout Europe. Tibi, who turned out be very well-informed, said that another invasion would lead to an outcry throughout the world, which the Soviet Union would want to avoid. I was also convinced that the countries of the West would not let us down.

It was next day, I think, when one of us had the idea of finding out what had happened to the building which everyone still called The Convent. It was rumoured that the State Security had left and that the building was empty.

'Let's go and see it before someone else takes it over,' I suggested.

'I wouldn't do it,' Tibi warned us, 'It might be dangerous. They could have left traps or even mines.'

Peter was not to be deterred. I too wanted to see the dreaded place. 'Are you coming?' we asked Tibi, who looked as if he'd rather not, but reluctantly agreed.

The gates were open. We advanced cautiously: Peter in front, then Tibi, followed by myself and Peter's wife, Vera. The doors were open and the building was as empty as a place can be from which the inhabitants have recently fled. It reminded me of the German flat in Koronovo to which the kindly Russian soldier had taken me on the day of my liberation. The lights had been left on in the corridor, and the office, into which we silently crowded, showed every sign of hasty departure, with overturned chairs, papers scattered over the floor, an empty cup on the typewriter.

As for the rest, I don't want to remember. They had been torturing people by locking them in cells so low that a man couldn't stand up in them, and so narrow that it was impossible to sit down. The stains on the floor were probably blood. Tibi was wandering around, mute, and in apparent shock. I returned to the office where Peter was reading a copy of a booklet from the top of a stack. 'It's about how to find out someone's real thoughts about the Party by questioning family members.' Tibi behaved as if he had never seen it before, yet decades later he turned out to have been one of the cruellest interrogators in the state Police.

10

In 1956, Hungary's immediate neighbours were the Soviet Union, Poland, Yugoslavia, Czechoslovakia and Austria. Of these, only Austria presented a door to the West. The border was guarded by an electrified fence, and the wide 'no man's land' was studded with landmines. The border guards in the watchtowers made sure that nothing bigger than a mouse could get across.

On October 23, 1956, many of the border guards were withdrawn in order to put down the Revolution. In the meantime, the Revolutionary forces were able to take up the landmines, and the exodus to Austria began.

Thirteen days later, the return of the Russians was followed by the collapse of the Revolutionary Army, and the retribution began, which lasted for many years. About five hundred people were executed, and thousands were imprisoned. At first, however, we were merely stunned by defeat. It was not only those involved in the fighting who were fleeing to Austria. Old and young, single and married, whole families debated whether to leave. They knew that once the border was again sealed, the prospect of escape might be lost for ever.

'Do you know what their plumbers earn? They get more over there than a surgeon does over here.'

'Over there' was *anywhere* beyond the Iron Curtain: Amsterdam, New Zealand, Buenos Aires, or Toronto.

'I've a second cousin in Chicago. I'm sure he'd put us up.'

'I've heard that, at Hyde Park Corner, you can say whatever you like without being arrested – even curse the government.'

'Once you're across the border, passports are no problem. I'm going to see the sea, and the Eiffel tower, and Japan.'

'No-one can take you away at the crack of dawn. They even have a saying in England that your home is your castle.'

Later, in Vienna, when I gave a peasant family the good news that they had been granted a visa for Belgium, they were not pleased. 'We want to go to America,' they insisted, 'Belgium is too far.'

Of course. Everyone had a distant uncle in America, but who had ever heard of Belgium?

It was the beginning of an avalanche. 'The Molnars are going!' 'The Kiss boy is already in Vienna and has sent word for his parents to follow!'

Rebellious adolescents didn't wait for parental approval but headed towards the border. 'I haven't told my Mum 'cause she wouldn't let me go. I don't care, I want freedom! And half the class is going.'

Freedom from fear, freedom from a government that intruded into every part of one's life, freedom to break the shackles which restrained us. More marriages broke up in a week than during the previous twelve months. Who would take the children: the one who went, or the one who stayed behind? Lovers who had parted came together again, and chose freedom abroad. Generations of Russians had tolerated a ban on travelling abroad – but ***we*** were a part of Europe, and couldn't bear the thought that should the barriers come down again, we would never see the world.

Whole villages were on the move like Birnam Wood to Dunsinane, painfully tearing up their roots. Those who were leaving were convinced that they would never be able to return, not even for a visit, and those who stayed were convinced that they would never get out again. Decisions were irrevocable. People simply handed over their keys to their neighbours, and left.

I certainly had no intention of emigrating. None of my friends did, however much they had been involved in the Revolution. For better or worse, this was our country, and Hungarian was our mother tongue. There was nothing a foreign land could offer in exchange for the poems reverberating in my head, for the wit of linguistic puns, for the joy of expressing myself with clarity. I'd read somewhere of a painter who was asked why he painted. 'Because I'm not a dog,' he replied, 'a dog can express every shade of emotion with his tail, but I have to use a brush.' I never tried to write poetry after my one youthful attempt – I had too much respect for it – but I was a clever rhyme-smith turning out comic verse in hexameters by the yard, since Hungarian yields easily to the classical forms. Speaking in German or

French would reduce communication to its basics. It would be like losing one's eyes and ears.

But my niece was already in Vienna with her husband, *en route* for Britain, and my sister and brother-in-law would soon be following them. They had thought of everything. My brother-in-law had been contacted by someone in the Party hierarchy who wanted their house. Since it was no longer customary to oust a family from its home on political grounds, and since the Comrade wanted the house for himself, he made an unofficial deal: a passport for the house. My sister would fly to Britain, their final destination, with a valid visa in her hand. But how could I live without her?

'We could probably include you in the deal,' she pleaded, 'You're young, you could start a new life there.'

'What sort of life? I'd probably be washing up in a cafe for the rest of my life. What else could I do in a foreign country, with no knowledge of the language?'

Never again would I wait for the cogwheel tram, never again have a cosy gossip with a friend in an *espresso*.Nowhere in the world was there the equivalent of a Budapest *espresso*, and, even if I learned the language, I would be crippled with a foreign accent for the rest of my life. But how could I live without my sister?

Then, I learnt about the gold ingots. They were buried under the woodpile at my brother-in-law's house, waiting for the time when owning them would no longer be a criminal offence. He couldn't leave them behind, and he and my sister had to go because they had my niece's baby boy with them. My niece and her husband had dared not expose the baby to the danger of a border crossing, so they had left him with his grandparents, until they too were able to come out. The gold would ensure their future, but it couldn't be hidden in luggage, which was likely to be searched at the railway terminal. And that was where I was to come in.

'Dani wants you to help him carry the gold into Austria,' Marinka said, 'It would make all the difference. At the age of forty-eight, I couldn't become a factory worker but, with the money, Dani could start a business.' She was right. I couldn't envisage my beloved sister slaving at a conveyor belt. The gold had to get to Austria.

'If there's a way out, there'll be a way back,' I said recklessly, as I agreed to help him. Weeks after the end of the Revolution, the land mines and electric fences had still not been replaced. Villagers near the border were making good money by escorting refugees across the dangerous territory, to be met by volunteers on the other side. Once Dani and I were safely across, I could return to Budapest.

'A harebrained scheme, if ever I saw one. You must be mad,' M. exclaimed, when I went to say goodbye to him, 'You won't come back,' he sighed.

'I will,' I promised faintly.

'My advice is not to leave Europe. It's your extended home. Further away, you'll find an alien world.'

'But I'm coming back,' I said, 'unless we get caught with the gold – which won't happen.'

A quick goodbye to Lili – just in case. What we were planning to do was dangerous, and the fewer who knew about it, the better. A few days later, Dani and I were on our way.

The shabby shopping bag, with a fortune in the bottom and with sandwiches on top, was surprisingly heavy. We carried it together to the terminal, which was buzzing with people waiting for the train. Men in shabby overcoats like Dani, women like me, with headscarves tied under their chin, peasant fashion, were anxiously getting on the morning train to Sopron, a town on the Austrian border.

We were to travel using different names, pretending not to know each other. Obtaining the necessary papers had not been difficult. A cottage industry, manufacturing documents, had sprung up again, just as it had twelve years ago when I had been part of the resistance. Dani had an additional affidavit from the central Post Office stating that his journey was essential.

The village before Sopron, the name of which I have forgotten, was too insignificant for the express train to stop at its station. As it began to slow down, the passengers on the seat opposite became agitated, and Dani, sitting next to them, turned pale. The train came to a halt with a jerk, and a dozen or more policemen came on, blocking the doors.

'Papers, please! Nobody leaves the train until we've seen your papers,' they shouted. Some of them seemed too young for the job. They must have been newly recruited to the force. They scrutinised everyone's documents.

'You are only going to Sopron to get across the border. You should be shot, the lot of you,' said the one who glanced at my not-very-good documents. Some people protested. 'All right,' he said, 'you'll be taken to the police station in Sopron, where they'll examine you papers more thoroughly. Until then, no-one leaves the train.'

They made an exception, however, for those whose journey was genuine. A young woman with a baby and an old man could prove they were residents of the village where the train had unexpectedly stopped. The old man was allowed to get off and shuffled away.

Dani, who had been in tight corners before, during Nazi times, didn't submit to the order. 'How dare you stop me?' he shouted, waving his documents, 'You'll get into trouble for this, I promise. Let me go at once.' His panic looked like righteous fury. The young policeman looked frightened and let him off the train.

All this happened in seconds. The shopping bag was under my feet. Could I hide it somewhere before I was found out? I looked around wildly and noticed that the old man was about to leave the station. I opened the window and shouted after him

'Hey, uncle! You left your shopping bag behind!'

He stopped, turned round, and looked at me uncertainly. I winked, offering him the bag through the window. 'You've forgotten this!'

I thought – if I was thinking at all – that Dani wouldn't have had time to leave the station. He would be lurking somewhere and would see the old man. I was right. Dani, as I later learned, grabbed the bag, went into the village, and soon found a guide to take him across the border.

The rest of us were escorted to the Police Headquarters in Sopron and, from there, to prison. Who cared! I could have sung and danced with relief, because smuggling bullion was a capital offence. Of the prison in Sopron, I can only recall that we bedded down on the floor, and that I took care of two small children whose mother was too distraught to look after them. In a day or two we were released. New waves of would-be refugees had arrived and there was simply not enough room for all of us.

I would like to tell a dramatic tale of how I eventually escaped in the middle of the night, stepping over land mines while a menacing wind howled through the trees. The truth is more prosaic. My brother-in-law had managed to negotiate passports for *all* of his family in exchange for the house. As a result, I left Hungary by train a few weeks later.